THE MAD, MAD, MAD, MAD SIXTIES COOKBOOK

MORE THAN 100 RETRO RECIPES FOR THE MODERN COOK

BY RICK RODGERS AND HEATHER MACLEAN

RUNNING PRESS
PHILADELPHIA • LONDON

© 2012 by Rick Rodgers and Heather Maclean
Photographs © 2012 by Ben Fink
Published by Running Press,
A Member of the Perseus Books Group

Books published by Running Press are available at special discounts for bulk purchases in the United States by corporations, institutions, and other organizations. For more information, please contact the Special Markets Department at the Perseus Books Group, 2300 Chestnut Street, Suite 200, Philadelphia, PA 19103, or call (800) 810-4145, ext. 5000, or e-mail special.markets@perseusbooks.com.

ISBN 978-0-7624-4573-8
Library of Congress Control Number: 2011944644

E-book ISBN 978-0-7624-4574-5

9 8 7 6 5 4 3 2 1
Digit on the right indicates the number of this printing

Cover design by Melissa Gerber
Interior design by Melissa Gerber
Edited by Jennifer Kasius
Typography: FT Master of Poster, Populaire Medium, Trade Gothic Std,
You Are Loved Pro, Tiki Holiday, Tiki Hut, and Tiki Island

Running Press Book Publishers
2300 Chestnut Street
Philadelphia, PA 19103-4371

Visit us on the web!
www.runningpress.com

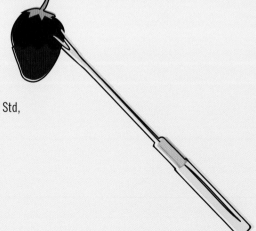

TABLE OF CONTENTS

INTRODUCTION: MARTINIS AND MEATBALLS 6

CHAPTER 1: PARTY LIKE A PLAYBOY 9

CHAPTER 2: FOOD TO DRINK BY: APPETIZERS AND HORS D'OEUVRES 17
Blini and Caviar 19
Clam Casino Dip 20
Oysters Rockefeller 21
Crab Rangoon 22
Deviled Eggs 24
Sweet and Tangy Meatballs 26
Real Onion Dip 28
Piggies in Blankets 30
Pimiento and Walnut Cheese Ball 32
Quiche Lorraine (or Julia) 34
Flower Drum Song Barbecued Ribs 36
Rumaki-a-rama 39
Shrimp Cocktail with Bloody Mary Sauce 42
Coconut Shrimp with Hot Chinese Mustard and Duck Sauce 43
Spam and Pineapple Kebabs 45
Eat-by-the-Barrel TV Mix 48

CHAPTER 3: VICHYSSOISE, ICEBERG, AND ASPIC . . . OH MY! SOUPS, SALADS, AND SANDWICHES 50
Tomato and Shrimp Aspic 51
Iceberg Lettuce Wedge with Blue Cheese Dressing and Bacon 54
Waldorf Salad 56
Manhattan Clam Chowder 57
Blender Gazpacho 58
Vichyssoise 60
Sixties Secret Grilled Cheese Sandwich 61
Cream of Tomato Soup 62
Date Nut Bread and Cream Cheese Sandwiches 65
Sloppy Joes 67
Stacked Salmon and Egg Salad Sandwich 69

CHAPTER 4: COMPANY FOOD: MAIN COURSES 72

Beef Wellington 74
Hungarian Goulash Gabor 78
Cold War Beef Stroganoff 79
Pan-Fried Steak with Butter 80
Yankee Pot Roast 81
The Ultimate Meat Loaf 84
Spaghetti and Meatballs Sophia 86
Souped-Up Swedish Meatballs 89
Puerto Rican Pork Chops with Mojo and Onions 90
Bangers and Mash 92
Baked Ham with Soda Pop Glaze 93
Leg of Lamb with Gravy and Mint Jelly 94
Miss Roaster Chicken 98
Potato Chip Baked Chicken 99
Soulful Fried Chicken 100
Chicken Divan 102
Chicken Breasts Kiev 104
Chicken à la King 106
Roast Turkey with Gravy 108
Not-Quite Fish Sticks 111
Duck à l'Orange 112
Shrimp Scampi 115
Crab-Stuffed Shrimp 116
Lobster Newberg 118
Matterhorn Fondue 120
"Don't Mess with Mom" Tuna and Noodle Casserole 122
Chile Rellenos Casserole 123

CHAPTER 5: BEST SUPPORTING PLAYERS: VEGETABLES AND SIDE DISHES 124

Asparagus aux Blender Hollandaise 125
Creamed Corn 126
Green Beans in Mushroom Sauce 128
Not-from-a-Box Macaroni and Cheese 130
Grandmother's Noodles with Sour Cream and Poppy Seeds 133
Potatoes au Gratin 134
Butter-Whipped Potatoes 135
Steakhouse Creamed Spinach 136
Candied Yams with Marshmallow Topping 137
Everyone Loves It Stuffing 138
Homemade Biscuits 139

Buttermilk Dinner Rolls 142

CHAPTER 6: SHOWSTOPPERS: DESSERTS 144

Tip Toe Inn's Lattice-Topped Cherry Cheesecake 146
Rocky Road Cupcakes 150
Pineapple Upside-Down Cake 153
Southern Caramel Cake 155
Soused Grasshopper Pie 157
Tart-Tongued Lemon Meringue Pie 161
Perfect Pie Dough 163
Nesselrode Pie 164
Daiquiri Lime and Gelatin Mold 166
Flaming Baked Alaska 168
Creamsicle Orange and Vanilla Cake 170
Secret Ingredient Two-Chip Cookies 172
Cherries Jubilee 173
Crêpes Bardot 174
Strawberries Romanoff 176

CHAPTER 7: EXECUTIVE COCKTAILS 178

Bloody Mary 183
Black Russian 184
Blue Hawaiian 185
Brandy Alexander 186
Daiquiri 188
Grasshopper 189
Mai Tai 190
Manhattan 192
Mint Julep 193
Martini, Very Dry 194
Negroni 197
Old-Fashioned 198
Screwdriver 201
Stinger 202
Tom Collins 203
Vodka Gimlet 204
Whiskey Sour 205

ACKNOWLEDGMENTS 207

A NOTE ON TRADEMARKS 208

INDEX 209

INTRODUCTION
MARTINIS AND MEATBALLS

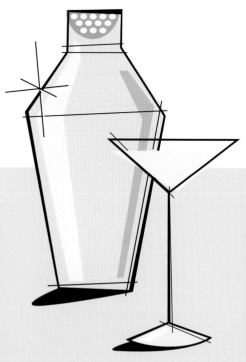

Whether you're a child of the Sixties or a child of parents shaped by them—we're one of each—the decade holds a special place in all of our hearts, returning frequently in movies and television series to redominate modern popular culture from dress and décor to dinner parties. We are referring to the era before the 1967 Summer of Love, the turning point when fashions changed from skinny ties to love beads, and the food on the table morphed from grasshopper pie to whole-wheat brownies (psychedelics optional).

We long for the time when Frank and the Rat Pack romanced us with their crooning, and everyone in the family could sit in front of the television and watch the same show without fear of Mom and Dad blushing. (Joey Heatherton on *The Hollywood Palace* was about as racy as things got.) The Vietnam War was hardly on anyone's radar, and Westerns provided most of the gunfire on TV. It was a time when there was more time; when you couldn't be reached by cell phone, text, or Twitter twenty-four hours a day. The workweek was shorter, weekends were sacred, and everyone was home for dinner.

Which bring us to the food. Just as the Sixties was an era of contradictions, so was its cuisine. Not that many people used *that* fancy word to describe their cooking! In the Fifties, mothers (for the lady of the house did the cooking while Dad worked) learned to embrace convenience foods, and many a formerly handmade dish was magically prepared with canned soup and frozen vegetables, and this trend carried over into the next decade. But, and this will be on your pop quiz, it was also when Julia Child introduced Americans to the fine art of cooking. She, and other "celebrity chefs" like James Beard (who had first been on television in

1946), proffered sumptuous recipes with simple instructions that anyone could follow. Julia illuminated the very modern idea that the journey of preparing food was as important and rewarding as eating it. The Sixties were actually the beginning of the gourmet movement in America.

In the Sixties, food wasn't something to just grab and eat on the run. It was a central part of social interaction, of personal and business development. The most important events in life unfurled across the lunch or dinner table. Relationships were made, mended, and mangled over food. Important clients were wooed, soothed, and sometimes lost at restaurants. And enough cannot be said of the Three-Martini Lunch.

The Mad, Mad, Mad, Mad Sixties Cookbook is here to joyously celebrate the decade's food, from fish sticks to Nesselrode pie. We understand that there may be some of you who still look askance at Sixties cooking. Maybe you remember things floating in gelatin that just didn't belong there. We promise you this: some of these recipes have kitsch value, but there is not one single thing in this book that we have not served to our friends and family with positive results. (Yes, even the canned soup recipes, which many people enjoyed as a walk down memory lane.)

We formally invite you to toss aside your preconceived notions of canned meat and convenience food and discover the scrumptious, sublime culinary heritage of the Sixties. Allow us to reintroduce you to authentic, epicurean delights like beef Wellington, chicken Kiev, and roast leg of lamb with neon-green mint jelly. Enjoy almost-forgotten international sensations (of dubious paternity) like vichyssoise and rumaki. Learn how to make a proper Sixties steak (in the pan, with butter). Of course, we'll still have some fun with picnic foods and pupu platters (makes us giggle every time). We double dog dare you to find something better than desserts you get to set on fire. And lest we forget, there is a more-than-complete selection of mixed drinks to wrap things up, including lots of tips on how to stir (or shake) up a mean cocktail.

With the recipes at hand, you will be serving supper like a Kennedy (Strawberries Romanoff), in a food coma thanks to childhood favorites (homemade Not-from-a-Box Macaroni and Cheese), and completely win over your aversion to aspic (well, maybe . . .). There are some dishes here that you will know already, but we strove to create recipes that are the very best versions you will ever have. And you will definitely know how to throw the best Sixties-themed party in your zip code. We promise.

In the interest of historical accuracy, we'll share how the dishes were prepared in the Sixties ("Kitchen Time Machine"), but since we know now about the evils of too much processed food (Cheez Whiz, we're looking at you . . .), we've elevated the recipes for the modern palate. Instead of just cracking open a can of tomato soup, we'll show you how to make it from scratch. Although instant onion soup mix was a staple in Sixties recipes, we chop fresh onions for our onion dip, and choose reduced-sodium broth over salty bouillon cubes, and so on. These are minor tweaks that will let you enjoy your meal all the more. But if you want to whip out the margarine or canned cream of mushroom soup for era authenticity, we'll tell you when, and how.

And true to the period, we'll have fun along the way. Ever wonder about the stories behind TV mix or onion soup dip? What made Warhol want to paint Campbell's soup cans? We'll give you enough food history and trivia to dazzle your diners while they enjoy your midcentury feast.

While we invite you to mix and match the dishes in this book, we also have provided party-ready menus. You'll be able to re-create everything from a "Mai Tai Madness" party with the best tropical food this side of the equator to a "Mint Julep Jamboree." (With these cocktail-centric menus, we are not promoting overdrinking! Always be sure to include plenty of nonalcoholic beverages too. But we do find that it is easier to serve a special single house cocktail than it is to turn your house into a fully stocked bar.) And we provide music playlists that are sure to set the mood.

So tie on an apron, pour yourself a drink, and get ready to rock and roll Sixties style!

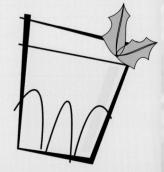

CHAPTER 1
PARTY LIKE A PLAYBOY

Before we delve into the delish, we have to set the scene. Parties in the Sixties had a definite element of class. Women wore pearls inside the house; men wore hats (outside and never indoors) and tipped them often as a sign of courtesy. Even the Playboy bunny logo wore a bow tie. Manners were very important, exemplified by the White House's chivalrous nickname: Camelot.

One of our most treasured possessions is a copy of *Betty Crocker's Hostess Cookbook* from 1967. Even though we know she's not real, we're still a little in love with Betty Crocker. Arguably the most successful corporate food spokesperson ever invented, Betty Crocker has been advising women on how to cook, bake, and hostess since 1921. She was created by a Minneapolis milling company (that would later become General Mills) to answer customers' letters about baking. "Betty" was chosen because it was a friendly name; "Crocker" was the last name of a recently retired executive. A secretary who won an internal contest among female employees created the signature Betty still uses today.

THE HOST(ESS) WITH THE MOST(EST)

Our favorite chapter in the spiral-bound *Betty Crocker's Hostess Cookbook*—besides "Gay Supper Parties"—is the advice for the "Hostess on Her Own": "No one will deny that the greatest asset any hostess can have is an obliging husband. But lacking this advantage, it's still possible for a girl on her own to earn her stripes as a party-giver"; as long as you "avoid a roast or bird that needs to be carved" as "this is really a man's domain." (We're guessing Gloria Steinem, even in her Playboy Bunny days, didn't have a lot of Betty Crocker parties. . . .) Hostesses (hosts, be damned!) are also reminded to stock up ashtrays ("There should be an ashtray, maybe two, on every table, chest, and sideboard—in fact, on every surface."), and to dress in "a simple costume"—"nothing too tight." Amen, Betty!

Here are some other suggestions . . . of our own:

DO . . . DRESS UP FOR DINNER

For any Sixties meal, big or small, dress as if you were going to eat at a fine restaurant—because you are! Even the most humble apartment can sub for the Four Seasons if you bring the right amount of elegance, attitude, and dress the part. No hats at the table, costume jewelry (if not actual pearls) are a must, and we highly recommend you invest in a few flirty or "Kiss the Cook" aprons.

DON'T . . . SERVE HUMONGOUS PORTIONS

The secret to staying slim back then was part girdle and part portion control. Since the Sixties, our standard serving size of everything from pasta to coffee has doubled, and our plates have kept pace. Dinnerware in the Sixties was 30 percent smaller than it is today. Like Volkswagen, think small.

DO . . . EXPECT THE UNEXPECTED (GUESTS)

When word gets out that you're having a Sixties party, expect the uninvited. If you prepare a couple extra entrées, you'll be sure to have enough for friends of friends who drop by unannounced.

DON'T . . . TRY AND DRINK LIKE A DRAPER

If you or your guests try and drink like you think they do on the Sixties-set television show *Mad Men*, your liver will not be amused. Like food portions, drinks have gotten supersized over the years. Sixties glasses were smaller and thinner, so each time an ad man knocked a straight-up martini back, it was only a percentage of what is typically served today. Today's martini glass averages eight to nine ounces; a cocktail glass in the Sixties held about five ounces when filled to overflowing. Allowing for filling the glass about four-fifths full, no matter how you do the math, there is a lot more booze in today's "up" drinks. And today's on-the-rocks glasses are pretty spacious too.

Actor Jon Hamm recently told Conan O'Brien about the perils of being recognized as *Mad Men*'s Don Draper when he's in a bar: "I get sent over bourbon in these tankers . . . human beings can't drink that much bourbon! I don't think they realize what I'm drinking on the show is not bourbon. It's tea, or water with food coloring in it."

Retro-sized Sixties barware will bring a big benefit to your cocktails: the smaller amount of liquid they hold is more likely to stay chilled while you drink it, which is how it was meant to be. In today's goldfish bowl–sized glasses, your martini is warm by the time you finish it. Look for the smaller glasses online or on the top shelf of your grandfather's bar in the rumpus room.

DO . . . COOK EXOTIC NEW THINGS

Don't know what makes a platter pupu? Never heard of rumaki? No matter. Most Sixties hosts hadn't either before they served them. Cooking in the Sixties meant taking risks and trying new things; mixing old and new. You may be a kitchen whiz and roll your own sushi, but you haven't lived until you've made a quivering, shimmering aspic.

SETTING THE TABLE

Of all the decades in the twentieth century, the Sixties—sandwiched between the kitschy Fifties and psychedelic Seventies—might be the easiest table to re-create. The look of Sixties serving ware was very clean. Solid colors were typically embellished with just circles, diamonds, or minimalist shapes. You will be able to pick up most of these items for a song at secondhand shops. Buying signed pieces at a reputable antiques dealer is another story, and a matter of personal taste. (We admit that we own some California Pottery pieces and a collection of Russel Wright dinnerware that set us back a bit.)

There are many places to find reasonably priced midcentury tableware. Secondhand shops, retro housewares shops, and online auction sites will offer a wide selection, and as long as you aren't looking for rare name brands, you should be able to affordably decorate your dining room for the affair. Here are some ideas to bring the Sixties home:

SILVER SERVINGWARE

Silver was a must for formal occasions. Most people began their collection as wedding presents. Dress up the table with shiny trays, buffets, and serving dishes. Of course, you don't have to use real silver; once there's food on top of them, your guests won't notice if you use sterling, aluminum, or even those silver-colored plastic serving items from discount stores. But do look for serving ware with a pretty pattern or angular Scandinavian design. Silverware with teak handles was all the rage. (And because so few homes had dishwashers, and everything was hand-washed, no one had to worry about wear and tear.)

CLASSIC WHITE AND CLEAR CRYSTAL

Brands like Lenox and Waterford still sell similar patterns today as they did in the midcentury. Look for intricate diamond cuts on crystal, and classic white china with subtle decoration.

GREEN OR AMBER GLASS

For a more casual meal, set the table with green- or amber-colored glass dishes. Popular Sixties pieces had diamond cuts or, our favorite, ruffled edges.

MILK GLASS

Invented in the sixteenth century, the opaque glass can be any number of colors, the solid white was the popular choice in the Sixties. Milk glass candy dishes, small bowls, vases, and salt and pepper shakers are easy to find in thrift stores or online. To mimic the midcentury look, go for anything with a "Hobnail" pattern—the raised bumps that are meant to imitate the look of lace.

CALIFORNIA POTTERY

Bright, solid-colored ceramic dishes were popular, and this brand of pottery from the West Coast set the standard. It can still be found online and at housewares stores specializing in retro fare. Sixties colors were vibrant: bright blue, green, orange, yellow, and gold. To this day, the sight of avocado green and harvest gold can conjure up memories of the era.

MODERN SCANDINAVIAN

Solid-colored enamel or porcelain with striking contrasting shapes—usually leaves—can still be found in stores. If you come across anything vintage by Cathrineholm, snap it up! But be warned, their fabulous pieces are often called "the gateway drug" to midcentury collecting mania.

TALL CANDLES AND ARTIFICIAL FLOWERS

Since fresh flowers (called "greenhouse flowers" back then) weren't available in every supermarket, and were considered a luxury purchase, most centerpieces revolved around tall candles. You can use either armed candelabras (a common wedding gift in the Sixties), or single stands.

That candle can look pretty lonely all by itself, so wreath it with an arrangement of plastic flowers. Don't feel restricted by the natural (more or less) colors of the flora. A secret weapon for midcentury decorators? Spray! Dull centerpieces were not tolerated. Fake frost was sprayed over winter items. Metallic spray paint was used to make food displays pop (gold pineapples, silver artichokes . . .). And clear spray just gave a nice sheen to otherwise dull walnuts or artificial daisies. Look for the various sprays at hobby supply shops.

TABLECLOTHS

Party linens, both tablecloth and linen napkins, were required for any social gathering. Depending on your menu, choose either a solid color matte tablecloth, or a retro pattern. A cut of fabric will also suffice; just don't use anything satiny or embroidered.

CHAFING DISH

No fair using a slow cooker—even the adorable little ones—to keep your food or sauces warm; they weren't invented until 1971. A chafing dish is the Sixties serving utensil of choice to keep your cocktail meatballs warm. It also acts as a cooking vessel for those flambé dishes that we promise to teach you how to make. You may find a simple inexpensive metal chafing dish or an elaborately stamped silver server that looks like something off King Louis XIV's table. Regardless of the style, you may have to do a bit of polishing to get your purchase up to snuff. Once you establish the kind of fuel it uses, buy plenty of it so you don't run out mid-cherries jubilee.

CHIP-AND-DIP SET

A Sixties party can attain pitch-perfect authenticity with just one item—a sleek chip-and-dip set. There are two styles. The first is a glass combination set, with a larger bowl for the chips, and a smaller container that hooks on the bowl's lip for the dip. They are easier to find than you might think, and because of their former ubiquity, reasonably priced. Or, go ceramic. If you can locate one, invest in a Brad Keeler chip-and-dip set. His shiny designs, mostly lettuce leaves with tomatoes or lobsters, are colorful conversation pieces that just might steal the show. If you have one, we're jealous. If you don't, good luck winning one on eBay! They are hot collectors' items.

COCKTAIL NAPKINS

Retro-style paper cocktail napkins are another easy way to set the tone for your party. Buy some to place at the bar area and near the food. Plan on having at least three cocktail napkins per person per hour of your party. If you are feeling flush, provide each guest with their own cloth cocktail napkin, a nicety that the toniest hostesses would employ. They are reusable too.

TINY TRASH CANS

There's nothing worse than not having a place to dispose of your used cocktail napkins. Placing them anywhere but a garbage can is completely unacceptable, unsanitary, and uncool. You don't have to drag your giant kitchen trash can into your party area. Just get a couple of bathroom-sized cans—in retro patterns if you can find them, if not, solid Sixties colors—and place a couple on the floor discreetly near the food.

TOOTHPICKS

Nothing says Sixties party like toothpicks with frilly, colored cellophane tips. Thankfully, they're still available at most grocery stores or easily found online. If you can find a vintage toothpick holder—usually a ceramic animal of some kind like a bunny hiding behind a tree stump or a piggy with an open back—definitely use it to present your toothpicks. If not, a small, plain shot glass will do.

ASHTRAYS

Even for modern nonsmokers, vintage ashtrays are great decoration. But during cocktail hour, they provide another use: a convenient receptacle for used toothpicks. Before the party starts, place a few toothpicks in each ashtray, and people will get the idea.

THE PLAYLIST

Back in the Sixties, about the best one could do was to stack a couple of records in the hi-fi changer and let them play in order. Now, thanks to the technology of CD and MP3 players, you can mix your party's background music with the push of a button or two, and have it play for hours and hours (or until the neighbors call the cops). With the reemergence of cocktail lounge music, the music selection is wide, varied, and readily available for purchase. We've provided some ideas for each of the party menus. We often prefer compilation CDs because they already offer a buffet of music with various talents to keep things lively.

You may not have to download and purchase your Esquivel or Yma Sumac. Check out the music channels on your cable TV or look for an online radio station that features midcentury music, and you just might find free tunes.

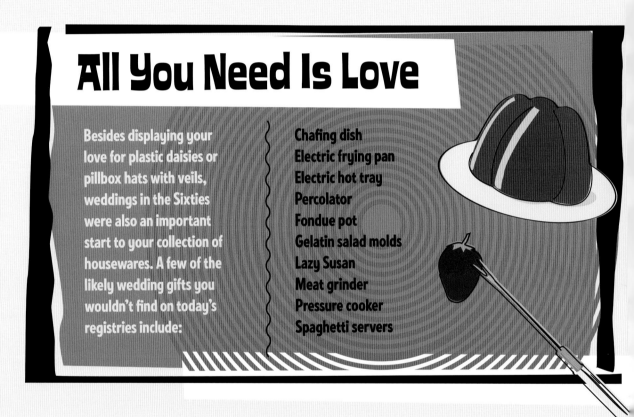

All You Need Is Love

Besides displaying your love for plastic daisies or pillbox hats with veils, weddings in the Sixties were also an important start to your collection of housewares. A few of the likely wedding gifts you wouldn't find on today's registries include:

Chafing dish
Electric frying pan
Electric hot tray
Percolator
Fondue pot
Gelatin salad molds
Lazy Susan
Meat grinder
Pressure cooker
Spaghetti servers

CHAPTER 2
FOOD TO DRINK BY: APPETIZERS AND HORS D'OEUVRES

◇◇

W hether you're trying to tide your guests over until dinner, or making sure they have something in their stomach while they knock back drinks, tiny food is big fun. Technically, "appetizers" are the first course of a meal, eaten with utensils while seated at the table. They are meant to complement the main course in terms of flavor, whetting the appetite for the starring attraction. "Hors d'oeuvres"— which means "apart from the main work" in French—are supposed to be separate food passed or situated around a gathering room before dinner. Most people use the terms interchangeably, and you can certainly serve both: hors d'oeuvres during the cocktail hour, and appetizers as the first course of your meal.

Ideally, hors d'oeuvres should be just one or two bites. How many different kinds should you serve, and how many per guest? If you have eight guests or less, two different hors d'oeuvres is perfect; shoot for three for parties up to twelve; four to however many you can manage for bigger blowouts. If you're serving dinner, you only need plan for six individual hors d'oeuvres per person. If it's cocktails-only, double that to twelve.

The most difficult part of serving hors d'oeuvres is planning. You don't want to be stuck in the kitchen all night. Balance your menu with hot and cold items, or ones that can be reheated in the oven without any fuss.

This is where dip comes into play as the party giver's best friend. Serve a big bowl of chips accompanied by a tasty dip, and you have just supplied a lot of servings with very little effort. Serve the combination in a retro chip-and-dip set, and you get extra points.

Most chefs recommend serving each type of hors d'oeuvre on its own tray or platter, but you can make beautiful presentations by lining up like-items. No matter what, never serve hot and cold hors d'oeuvres on the same plate.

Put Your Right Hand Out

Raise your hand if you love getting a slimy, wet handshake at a cocktail party. Yeah, we don't either. Though it might seem like a difficult juggling act, a good party guest balances all their food and drink in their left hand, leaving their right hand free for dry, well-mannered greetings.

To do this, tuck a small fold of the middle of your cocktail napkin in between your left hand ring finger and pinkie. Spread the rest of the napkin out, and place your hors d'oeuvre on it. Now hold your glass by the bottom against the flat of your palm between your thumb and forefinger, steadying the sides with those fingers. It sounds complicated on paper, but try it and you'll see how easy it is to be a perfect party guest.

BLINI AND CAVIAR

Blini and caviar, popularized by their appearance at Russian-esque upscale restaurants like New York's Russian Tea Room, were the ultimate indicator of midcentury luxury. The little pancakes are simple to make at home. You can serve them with caviar or smoked salmon. And, as a boon to the busy party giver, they should not be hot—that would only warm the caviar.

¾ cup all-purpose flour
⅔ cup buckwheat flour
¼ teaspoon salt
1¼ cups whole milk
½ cup full-fat sour cream, plus more for serving
2 large eggs
4 tablespoons (½ stick) unsalted butter, melted and slightly cooled
Vegetable oil, for cooking
2 ounces caviar
Minced onion, minced hard-boiled egg yolk, and minced fresh chives, for serving

1. Sift the flour, buckwheat flour, and salt together into a medium bowl. Whisk the milk, sour cream, eggs, and butter together in another bowl. Add to the flour mixture and whisk just until smooth. Do not overmix.

2. Heat a griddle or large skillet over medium heat until a splash of water forms tiny bubbles that dance on the griddle surface. Lightly oil the griddle. Using a tablespoon for each, spoon the batter onto the griddle. Cook until the underside is golden brown, about 1 minute. Turn and cook until the other sides are browned, about 1 minute more. Transfer to a plate. (The blini can be prepared, cooled, covered, and stored at room temperature, for 8 hours before serving.)

3. Place the caviar in a small serving bowl and nestle in a larger bowl of ice. (Or, if you have a caviar server, use it.) Serve the blini with the caviar and the sour cream, onion, egg yolk, and chives.

CLAM CASINO DIP

Onion dip was king of the chip-and-dip set, but clam dip also had plenty of supporters. Our version is dressed up with the flavors of another Sixties fave: clams casino—baked clams seasoned with red peppers and bacon. Like many midcentury classics, it relies on canned food. If you have fond memories of Mom's clam dip, we provide the recipe in the "Kitchen Time Machine."

1 large red pepper
2 (6.5-ounce) cans minced clams
8 ounces cream cheese, at room temperature
1 teaspoon dried oregano
½ teaspoon Worcestershire sauce
Hot red pepper sauce
2 strips bacon, cooked until crisp, drained and finely chopped
Potato chips, preferably ridged, for serving

1. Position a broiler rack about 8 inches from the source of heat and preheat the broiler. Broil the pepper, turning occasionally, until the skin is blackened and blistered, about 8 minutes. Transfer to a bowl and let cool. Remove and discard the skin. Chop into ¼-inch dice. Measure ½ cup and set aside. Reserve the remaining red pepper for another use.

2. Drain the clams and reserve 2 tablespoons of the juice. Using a rubber spatula, mash the cream cheese with the juice in a medium bowl. Stir in the drained clams, red pepper, oregano, and Worcestershire sauce. Season with the hot red pepper sauce. Cover and refrigerate until chilled, at least 2 hours and up to 1 day.

3. Transfer to a serving bowl and sprinkle with the bacon. Serve chilled, with the chips for dipping.

KITCHEN TIME MACHINE

For Classic Clam Dip, drain 2 (6.5-ounce) cans minced clams, and reserve 2 tablespoons of the clam juice. Mash 8 ounces softened cream cheese, with the juice, 1 small minced garlic clove, 1 teaspoon Worcestershire sauce, and 1 teaspoon fresh lemon juice, and season with hot red pepper sauce. Cover and refrigerate for at least 2 hours and up to 1 day.

OYSTERS ROCKEFELLER

MAKES 24 OYSTERS

Although invented at Antoine's Restaurant in New Orleans in the late 1800s, we include these rich, hot oysters because of Nelson Rockefeller's influence on New York life in the Sixties, and they were a popular way to start a meal during the decade. We warn you—they are as rich as Rockefeller, which is how they got their name. How many is too many? Three of these luscious oysters is enough for most people, especially as a first course, but many restaurants serve six to twelve per plate.

1 (10-ounce) box frozen chopped spinach, thawed
8 tablespoons unsalted butter, divided
1 medium celery rib, very finely minced
4 scallions, white and green parts, very finely minced
2 tablespoons anise-flavored liqueur, such as Herbsaint or Pernod (but not anisette)
½ teaspoon Worcestershire sauce
¼ cup Italian-seasoned dried bread crumbs
Hot red pepper sauce
24 oysters, shucked, curved shells served

1. A handful at a time, squeeze the excess water from the spinach. Set the spinach aside.

2. Heat 1 tablespoon of butter in a medium skillet over medium heat. Add the celery and cook until softened, about 1 minute. Add the scallions and cook, stirring often, until very tender but not browned, about 3 minutes. Add the liqueur and cook until it evaporates, about 15 seconds. Stir in the spinach and cook, stirring often, until the mixture is dry, about 1 minute. Remove from the heat. Cut the remaining butter into tablespoons, and add to the skillet. Stir until the butter is melted. Add the Worcestershire sauce, then the bread crumbs. Season with hot red pepper sauce. Set aside at room temperature. (The green butter can be made up to 1 day ahead, cooled, covered, and refrigerated. Remove from the refrigerator 1 hour before using.)

3. Position a broiler rack 6 inches from the source of heat and preheat the broiler. Crumple aluminum foil in a broiler pan to make a bed for the oysters. (You may need two broiler pans or rimmed baking sheets to hold all 24 oysters.)

4. Nestle the oysters, in their shells, in the foil. Spoon about 1 tablespoon of the butter mixture over each oyster. Broil until the butter is bubbling and the edges of the oysters are curling, about 3 minutes. Transfer the oysters to dinner plates and serve hot.

CRAB RANGOON

Surely nothing like crab Rangoon ever existed in Burma or even Polynesia. Once a mainstay of the pupu platter, crab Rangoon isn't as popular as it used to be, perhaps because it must be deep-fried to appreciate it in its crispy-creamy-crabby glory. Newer, baked versions just aren't the same.

4 ounces cream cheese, at room temperature
2 teaspoons soy sauce
1 scallion, white and green parts, minced
1 garlic clove, minced
4 ounces crabmeat, picked over for cartilage
Hot red pepper sauce
Cornstarch, for dusting
24 wonton squares (from half a 12-ounce package)
1 large egg white, beaten with a pinch of salt until foamy, for sealing the wontons
Vegetable oil, for deep-frying
Hot Chinese Mustard (page 43) and duck sauce, for serving

1. Mash the cream cheese, soy sauce, scallion, and garlic together in a medium bowl with a rubber spatula. Stir in the crabmeat. Season with the hot red pepper sauce.

2. Line a baking sheet with waxed paper and dust it with cornstarch. Place a wonton in front of you, with the points facing north, south, east, and west. Brush the edges with a little egg white. Place a teaspoon of the filling in the lower half of the wonton. Fold the north tip over to meet the south tip, and press the open sides closed. Press the filling in the wonton to spread and flatten it slightly. Fold the east and west tips to meet in the center of the wonton and seal them together with a dab of egg white. Place on the baking sheet. Repeat with the remaining filling and wontons. Cover loosely with plastic wrap and refrigerate until ready to cook, up to 2 hours.

3. Position a rack in the center of the oven and preheat the oven to 200°F. Line a baking sheet with a brown paper bag.

4. Pour enough oil into a deep, heavy saucepan to fill halfway up the sides. Heat over high heat to 350°F on a

deep-frying thermometer. In batches without crowding, add the wontons and deep-fry, turning the wontons as needed, until golden brown, about 2 minutes. Using a wire spider or a slotted spoon, transfer the wontons to the brown paper-lined baking sheet and keep warm in the oven while frying the remaining wontons.

5. Transfer to a serving platter and serve warm with the hot mustard and duck sauce.

Talking Tiki

Tiki culture, a romanticized mix of Polynesian and Pacific Rim food and tropical décor took all of America by storm when soldiers stationed overseas returned from World War II. Spurred by the national success of tiki-themed restaurants Don the Beachcomber and Trader Vic's, by the time Hawaii became the fiftieth state in 1959, it was in full luau.

Even when home parties in the Sixties didn't have a full-on tiki theme, tiki elements were usually included at the beginning with bamboo-decorated bars, tropical drinks like Mai Tais, cocktail umbrellas, and pupu platters.

Tiki culture was eventually eclipsed by rock and roll and disco, but enjoyed a renaissance in the late 1990s with the advent of Pacific Rim fusion cooking and SpongeBob SquarePants, a guy who really appreciated all things Tiki.

MILESTONES IN MIDCENTURY TIKI CULTURE

1958—*South Pacific* bows at the movie box office.
1961—*Blue Hawaii*, the first of Elvis's three Hawaii movies opens.
1962—*Girls Girls Girls!* starring Elvis and shot in Hawaii opens.
1963—The Enchanted Tiki Room opens at Disneyland.
1964—*Gilligan's Island* debuts on CBS.
1965—Hawaiian pop singer Don Ho releases his first album.
1966—*Elvis's Paradise, Hawaiian Style* opens.
1968—*Hawaii Five-O* debuts on CBS.

DEVILED EGGS

Deviled eggs should have a little kick to them—just how devilishly hot is determined by how hard you shake the hot pepper sauce bottle. Make deviled eggs for an alfresco picnic, as cocktail party fare, or to start off a holiday supper with relatives. To keep your hard-boiled eggs from acquiring that unattractive grey-green ring around the yolks, avoid overcooking. In fact, our method for hard-boiled eggs skips the boiling altogether. Personalize your deviled eggs with garnishes of chopped olives or pimiento, or a sprinkle of minced fresh parsley or chives.

1 dozen large eggs
½ cup mayonnaise
1 scallion, white and green parts, minced
1 small celery rib, minced
¼ teaspoon hot red pepper sauce, or more to taste
Salt
Paprika, preferably hot paprika, for garnish

1. Place the eggs in a single layer in a large saucepan. Add enough cold water to cover the eggs by ½ inch. Bring to a simmer (the pot will be filled with small bubbles) over high heat. Remove from the heat and cover. Let stand for 15 minutes. Using a slotted spoon, transfer the eggs to a bowl of iced water. Let stand until the eggs are chilled, about 20 minutes.

2. Crack and peel the eggs. Cut each egg in half lengthwise. Remove the egg yolks and reserve the whites. Rub the egg yolks with a rubber spatula through a coarse wire sieve into a medium bowl. Stir in the mayonnaise, scallion, and celery. Add the hot red pepper sauce. Season with salt, and more hot sauce, if desired.

3. Transfer the yolk mixture to a pastry bag fitted with a ½-inch-wide fluted pastry tip. Pipe the mixture into the egg whites. (You can also simply spoon the mixture into the whites. Or transfer the yolk mixture into a plastic storage bag, snip off one corner of the bag, and use as an impromptu pastry bag.) Arrange the eggs, filled sides up, in a shallow dish. Sprinkle with the paprika. Cover with plastic wrap and refrigerate until chilled, at least 1 hour. (The eggs can be made up to 2 days ahead.) Serve chilled.

SWEET AND TANGY MEATBALLS

These betcha-can't-eat-just-one cocktail meatballs belong firmly in the era of convenience foods, and try as we might, we haven't come up with a better sauce. The sauce will also coat 2 pounds of miniature smoked cocktail sausages, cooked under a broiler for a few minutes until sizzling. And we know lots of folks who buy frozen meatballs at a wholesale club and mix them into the sauce for the easiest hors d'oeuvres ever.

Vegetable oil for the baking sheet
1 pound ground round beef
1 cup fresh bread crumbs (whirl sliced bread in a blender)
1 large egg, beaten
¼ cup minced onion
2 tablespoons milk
1 garlic clove, minced
1 teaspoon salt
¼ teaspoon freshly ground black pepper
¾ cup ketchup-style chili sauce
¾ cup grape jelly
½ teaspoon hot red pepper sauce
Wooden toothpicks, for serving

1. Preheat the oven to 350°F. Line a rimmed baking sheet with aluminum foil, and oil the foil.

2. Mix the ground beef, bread crumbs, egg, onion, milk, garlic, salt, and black pepper together in a large bowl (your hands work best). Shape into 36 small meatballs. Arrange on the baking sheet. Bake until browned, about 20 minutes. Drain off any fat. (The meatballs can be made, cooled, and stored in a plastic bag, up to 2 days ahead.)

3. Meanwhile, bring the chili sauce, grape jelly, and hot red pepper sauce to a simmer in a large saucepan over medium heat. Simmer, stirring often, until lightly thickened, about 10 minutes. Add the meatballs and cook, stirring occasionally, until heated through, about 5 minutes.

4. Transfer the meatballs and sauce to a chafing dish (or fondue pot), to keep warm during serving. Serve warm, with wooden toothpicks to spear the meatballs.

Food A Go-Go

In the Sixties, newfound wealth, mobility, and the desire for cosmopolitan food drove people to dine out more than ever before. The "exotic" choices of the day? French, Italian, and Japanese restaurants.

You can still visit some of the most popular restaurants of the day that opened in the 1960s and still serve up plenty of atmosphere and delicious entrees, including:

- La Grenouille, New York
- The Monocle, Washington DC
- Dan Tana's, Los Angeles
- Maxim's, Chicago

Chain Meal

A few of today's reigning national chain restaurants also got their start in the Sixties, and are still going strong:

- Benihana
- TGI Fridays
- Red Lobster
- Red Robin
- Old Spaghetti Factory
- Cracker Barrel
- Wendy's
- Domino's Pizza
- Taco Bell
- Arby's
- Subway

REAL ONION DIP

Thanks to the advent of sturdier "ruffled" potato chips that didn't explode when you touched them, very few parties in the Sixties were without a bowl of onion dip. And why not? Is there an easier way to feed a crowd? Mix sour cream with powdered onion soup. Serve. We love the original (and we'll give it to you below), but we couldn't help but elevate it by making it from scratch with caramelized onions. So get out the chip-and-dip set and dig in!

2 tablespoons vegetable oil

3 medium yellow onions, chopped

1 pint sour cream; divided

¾ cup (3 ounces) crumbled blue cheese; divided

Salt and freshly ground black pepper

Chopped fresh parsley or chives, for garnish (optional)

Potato chips, preferably ridged, for serving

1. Heat the oil in a large skillet over medium-high heat. Add the onions and cook, stirring occasionally, until beginning to brown, about 6 minutes. Reduce the heat to medium-low. Cook, stirring often, until the onions are deep golden brown, about 30 minutes.

2. Remove from the heat. Add ½ cup sour cream to the skillet and scrape up the browned bits with a wooden spoon. Transfer to a medium bowl. Add ¼ cup of blue cheese to the bowl and stir it in to partially melt the cheese. Let cool completely.

3. Stir in the remaining sour cream and blue cheese. Season with salt and pepper. Cover and refrigerate until chilled, at least 2 hours or up to 2 days.

4. Sprinkle with the chives, if using, and serve chilled, with the potato chips.

KITCHEN TIME MACHINE

Mix one 16-ounce container of sour cream with one 1-ounce envelope of dry onion soup mix in a medium bowl. Return to the sour cream container and cover. Refrigerate until the onions soften, at least 1 hour and up to 2 days. Serve chilled.

California Dip

Lipton's Onion Soup, basically dehydrated onions and seasonings in a packet, debuted in 1952. Two years later, an anonymous housewife married the soup with sour cream to make a dip for chips. The recipe took off like briquettes soaked with lighter fluid, and by 1958, it was printed on the back of every Lipton's box. No one is quite sure about the California reference. Was the inventor from California, or did the dip acquire the name to evoke visions of patio parties around a turquoise-blue, chlorinated built-in pool? The world may never know.

PIGGIES IN BLANKETS

MAKES 40 PIGGIES, ABOUT 10 SERVINGS

When big franks are wrapped in dough, they are called pigs in blankets. When small cocktail wieners are wrapped in dough, they are piggies in blankets. We use freshly prepared buttermilk dough for our piggies, and we can tell you that the effort will be worth it when you hear your friends snorting with pleasure. But we also include a recipe for pigs with store-bought refrigerated croissant dough, the product that introduced Poppin' Fresh, the Pillsbury Doughboy, to the world. (We really wanted to name these Chauvinist Pigs in Blankets, but our research showed that the term didn't take hold until the early Seventies. So call them what you wish!)

Flour, for rolling out the dough
½ batch Buttermilk Dinner Rolls (page 142)
1 (14-ounce package) (about 40) miniature "cocktail" beef franks or smoked sausages
¾ cup Dijon mustard
¼ cup honey

1. Position a rack in the center of the oven and preheat the oven to 350°F.
2. Roll out the dough on a lightly floured work surface into a 15-by-4-inch rectangle. Using a yardstick and a pizza wheel, cut into forty 1 ½-inch squares. For each piggie, place a dough square in front of you with the points facing north, south, east, and west. Place a frank horizontally in the center of the square with its tips facing east-west. Bring the north and south tips together to meet over the center of the frank and press them closed, with the ends of the frank peeking out from the dough. Arrange the piggies on an ungreased baking sheet, open side up. Cover with a kitchen towel and let stand in a warm place until the dough looks slightly puffed, 20 to 30 minutes.
3. Bake until the dough is golden brown, about 15 minutes. (The piggies can be made up to 2 hours ahead, stored at room temperature. For longer storage, transfer to a plastic storage bag and refrigerate for up to 1 day. Reheat on an aluminum-foiled covered baking sheet in a preheated 350°F oven for about 10 minutes.)
4. Meanwhile, mix the mustard and honey together in a small bowl. Transfer to a serving platter. Serve warm, with the mustard for dipping.

KITCHEN TIME MACHINE

Open an 8-ounce package of refrigerated crescent rolls and separate into 8 triangles. For each, wrap a dough triangle around a standard frankfurter, leaving the ends of the frankfurter exposed and pressing the seams in the dough closed. Place on an ungreased baking sheet. Do not cover and let the dough rise before baking. Bake in a preheated 375°F oven until the dough is golden brown, about 12 minutes. Cut each frank into thirds. Omit the Dijon mustard-honey mixture, and serve hot with prepared yellow mustard for dipping. Makes 24 pigs, about 8 servings.

PIMIENTO AND WALNUT CHEESE BALL

MAKES 12 SERVINGS

Plain pimiento cheese, as many a Southerner will tell you, is a heaven-sent sandwich filling. Here it is transformed into a spread to grace your favorite snack cracker. (We're thinking Triscuits. . . .) Pimientos may look similar to red bell peppers, but they are really different. The latter have a spicier flavor. Pimientos are mild, and even though Spain leads in world production, they seem about as European as Andy Williams.

1 (8-ounce) package cream cheese, well softened
2 cups (8 ounces) shredded sharp or mild Cheddar
¼ cup mayonnaise
1 teaspoon Worcestershire sauce
1 (4-ounce) jar chopped pimientos, drained, rinsed, and patted dry
Hot red pepper sauce
1½ cups (6 ounces) finely chopped walnuts
Crackers, for serving

1. Mash the cream cheese, Cheddar, mayonnaise, and Worcestershire sauce together with a rubber spatula in a medium bowl. Mix in the pimientos. Season with hot red pepper sauce.

2. Scrape the cheese mixture onto a large sheet of plastic wrap. Bring the wrap up to cover the cheese, and twist the ends together to shape the cheese mixture into a ball. Refrigerate until chilled and firmer, at least 2 hours. (The cheese ball can be prepared up to 5 days ahead.)

3. Just before serving, unwrap the ball and roll in the walnuts to cover. Place on a serving platter. Serve chilled or at room temperature, with the crackers.

QUICHE LORRAINE (OR JULIA)

MAKES 8 SERVINGS

Julia Child's biggest contribution to French cooking was making it easy to understand. Until she arrived on the scene in the early Sixties, only the gourmet-crazed would know what a quiche was . . . or how to pronounce it. But down-to-earth, clarion-voiced Julia changed all that with her can-do approach to the most complicated recipes. This version harks back to before quiche became a cliché. It's slightly Americanized, baked in a pie plate and not a tart or quiche pan, and best enjoyed with a glass of Chablis (preferably not out of a jug).

All-purpose flour, for rolling out the dough
Perfect Pie Dough (page 163)
6 bacon strips
4 large eggs
2 cups half-and-half
¼ teaspoon salt
¼ teaspoon freshly ground black pepper
1 large pinch freshly grated nutmeg
1 cup (4 ounces) shredded Gruyère or Swiss cheese

1. Roll out the dough on a lightly floured work surface into a 12-inch-diameter round about ⅛ inch thick. Transfer to a 9-inch pie plate, letting the excess dough hang over the sides. Fold the dough under so the edge of the fold is flush with the edge of the pie plate rim. Flute the dough or lightly press a fork around the edge of the dough to decorate it. Freeze the uncovered pastry-lined pie plate for 15 to 30 minutes.

2. Position a rack in the lower third of the oven and preheat the oven to 400°F.

3. Meanwhile, cook the bacon in a large skillet over medium heat until crisp and browned, about 8 minutes. Transfer to paper towels to cool. Coarsely chop the bacon.

4. Pierce the pastry all over (in about 10 places) with a fork. Top the entire pastry with a sheet of aluminum foil and fill with pastry weights (see Note on opposite page). Place on a baking sheet. Bake until the edges of the pastry are set and beginning to brown, about 12 minutes. Remove the pie plate on the baking sheet from the oven. Lift off the foil with the weights.

5. Whisk the eggs, half-and-half, salt, pepper, and nutmeg together in a medium bowl. Sprinkle the bacon and Gruyère in the pie plate. Pour in the egg mixture. Return to the oven and reduce the oven temperature to 325°F. Continue baking until the filling is evenly puffed and golden brown, about 35 minutes.

6. Transfer to a wire cake rack and let cool 10 minutes. Slice and serve warm or cooled to room temperature.

NOTE: You will need ceramic or aluminum pastry weights (available at kitchenware shops or online) to weight the dough during its initial baking. Or, you can save some money and just use a pound of dried beans as weights. The dried beans can be stored for another few uses, but after six months or so, they can get a little funky and will need to be replaced.

Free Fat

Like lard, bacon fat adds flavor to the most simply-cooked dishes. In the Sixties, pot roasts were seared in it, chicken was fried in it, and even salad dressings were made from it. Because bacon was cooked every morning in millions of homes, bacon fat accumulated pretty quickly, and most cooks saved it. The common receptacle was a coffee can stored in a cool, dark place, either the refrigerator or under the sink. To try cooking with some of that Sixties goodness, whenever you make bacon at home, save the fat. Just cool it a bit, pour into a covered jar, and refrigerate for up to 2 months. You'll thank us when it comes to Soulful Fried Chicken (page 100)!

FLOWER DRUM SONG BARBECUED RIBS

MAKES 6 TO 8 SERVINGS

Rodgers and Hammerstein's *Flower Drum Song* may have been a Broadway hit in the late 1950s (the film version came out in 1961), but its depiction of life in San Francisco's Chinatown still informed the cultural consciousness of the early Sixties. Just as the musical may not have been authentic, it was tasty . . . much like these barbecued ribs. They are the kind of sweet and sticky ribs that you found (and may still find) on every Chinese restaurant's menu.

2½ to 3 pounds baby back ribs, cut into 3 slabs

⅔ cup tomato ketchup

¼ cup packed light brown sugar

1 large egg, beaten

2 tablespoons soy sauce

2 tablespoons dry sherry

3 garlic cloves, minced

½ teaspoon salt

1 large pinch of ground cinnamon

1 large pinch of ground cloves

1½ teaspoons baking soda

Vegetable oil, for the broiler rack

1. Bring a large pot of lightly salted water to a boil over high heat. Add the ribs and cook for 2 minutes. Drain and rinse under cold running water. Let cool.

2. Whisk the ketchup, brown sugar, egg, soy sauce, sherry, garlic, salt, cinnamon, and cloves together in a medium bowl. Add the baking soda—the mixture will foam. Layer the ribs and ketchup marinade in a glass or ceramic baking dish. Cover with plastic wrap and refrigerate, occasionally turning the ribs in the marinade for at least 3 and up to 8 hours.

3. Position a rack in the lower third of the oven and preheat the oven to 450°F.

4. Line a broiler pan with aluminum foil. Place a broiler rack in a pan and lightly oil the rack. Remove the

ribs from the marinade, letting the excess marinade drip off. Transfer the marinade to a small bowl, cover, and refrigerate. Arrange the ribs, meaty side up, on the rack. Pour about 2 cups hot tap water into the roasting pan, being sure the water doesn't reach the rack. Roast until the sauce starts to caramelize in spots, about 20 minutes. Turn the ribs and brush with some of the reserved marinade. Roast until the sauce starts to caramelize, about 20 minutes. Turn again, and brush with the marinade, discarding the remaining marinade. Roast until the ribs are tender when pierced with a meat fork and the sauce is reduced to a lightly caramelized glaze, about 25 minutes more. If the water evaporates, add more. If the ribs get too dark, tent the broiler pan with aluminum foil.

5. Transfer the ribs to a carving board and let stand for 5 minutes. Cut between the ribs, transfer to a platter, and serve warm.

I Want My Baby Back

Baby back ribs are a relatively recent addition to the butcher's case. Cut from the same bones found on a pork loin roast, they have very tender, succulent meat. Spareribs are meatier, but tougher and with more fat and gristle, but they are the only ribs that Chinese restaurants would have used until baby backs appeared on the scene.

To use spareribs, buy 3 pounds of St. Louis-style ribs, which have had the extraneous meaty flap trimmed off to make a neat, rectangular slab of ribs. Cut the ribs into 3 or 4 slabs. Cover the broiler pan with aluminum foil to create steam to help tenderize the gristle, and roast for 30 minutes. Turn the ribs, brush with marinade, and roast uncovered for 30 minutes. Then turn again, brush with the marinade, and roast until tender, about 40 minutes more, tenting the ribs with foil as needed.

At a Chinese restaurant, the individual ribs would have been chopped across the bone into smaller chunks with a cleaver. If you have a cleaver, and are feeling assured, you can chop the ribs. If appropriate, sing "I Enjoy Being a Girl" while doing so.

RUMAKI-A-RAMA

MAKES ABOUT 3 DOZEN, 9 TO 12 SERVINGS

Japanese-inspired rumaki, a popular addition to the Sixties pupu platter, is made by wrapping chicken livers in bacon and marinating them in a sweet soy sauce before broiling. Since chicken livers aren't a modern fave, you can also make rumaki with date or pineapple chunks, as we detail below. You're welcome.

18 bacon slices (about 1 pound), cut in half crosswise to make 36 pieces
½ cup soy sauce
2 tablespoons honey
1 scallion, white and green parts, minced
1 tablespoon peeled and minced fresh ginger
1 garlic clove, minced
¼ teaspoon freshly ground black pepper
18 chicken livers, trimmed and cut in half crosswise to make 36 pieces
18 large pitted dates, cut in half crosswise (optional)
36 fresh pineapple chunks, about ¾-inch square (optional)
36 water chestnut slices
36 wooden toothpicks, soaked in water for 30 minutes, drained

1. Position racks in the center and upper third of the oven and preheat the oven to 400°F. Arrange the bacon on two rimmed baking sheets. Bake until the bacon gives off its fat and is beginning to brown, about 8 minutes. Transfer the parcooked bacon to a plate and let cool. (Pour the bacon fat into a covered container and refrigerate for another use if desired.)

2. Whisk the soy sauce, honey, scallion, ginger, garlic, and pepper in a small bowl to dissolve the garlic. For each rumaki, spear a piece of liver (or date half or pineapple chunk) onto a drained toothpick with a water chestnut slice, and wrap with a parcooked bacon half slice. Place in a shallow glass or ceramic baking dish, and pour in the soy sauce mixture. Cover and refrigerate, turning the rumaki occasionally in the marinade, for at least 2 and up to 6 hours.

3. Position a broiler rack about 6 inches from the source of heat and preheat the broiler. Lightly oil a broiler rack.

4. Drain the rumaki. Arrange on the broiler rack. Broil, turning occasionally, until the bacon is browned and the chicken livers are cooked to medium, about 5 minutes. If the rumaki are scorching, move the broiler rack to a lower rung. Serve warm.

Perfect Rumaki

There are a couple of tricks to getting rumaki right:

- Precook the bacon to be sure that it cooks up nice and crispy in the broiler.

- Soak the toothpicks in water before assembling the rumaki so they don't burn during broiling. If the toothpicks still scorch, replace them with fresh toothpicks before serving.

- Rumaki ingredients are slippery devils, so find a method of assembly that works for you. Here's how we do it: About $1/2$ inch from the end of the bacon slice, spear the slice with a toothpick. Now pierce the water chestnut through its center onto the toothpick, followed by a liver chunk. Wrap the long end of the bacon around the liver and water chestnut, spearing the opposite end of the bacon on the toothpick. Don't worry about any loose bacon, as it will shrink up when cooked.

KITCHEN TIME MACHINE

Substitute ½ teaspoon ground ginger and ¼ teaspoon garlic powder for the fresh ginger and garlic.

The Straight Pupu

From the Hawaiian word *pūpū*, which means a relish or appetizer, pupu platters originated in America in the 1930s at California restaurants, and they are still available today in many Chinese restaurants. While the food is meant to be an amalgam of Polynesian flavors, it generally consists of Americanized Cantonese and Japanese food.

A pupu platter (a bowl with compartments for the separate appetizers) is another item that is easy to find online and will add some Sixties sass to your party. The platter usually has a hole in the center to hold a small hibachi grill, but none of our recipes require tableside cooking (although you could use the hibachi to briefly reheat the food).

If you don't have an "official" pupu platter (a wooden bowl), there are many compartmentalized appetizer servers that would still do the trick. In *the* exception to the each-hors-d'oeuvre-gets-its-own-tray rule, everything on the pupu platter should be served together, usually around a large pineapple, an assortment of tiki statues, or a small hibachi grill.

Pupu Platter: From top right, Spam and Pineapple Kebobs (page 45); Crab Rangoon (page 22); Coconut Shrimp (page 43); Rumaki-a-Rama (page 39); and Flower Drum Song Barbecue Ribs (page 36).

SHRIMP COCKTAIL WITH BLOODY MARY SAUCE

MAKES 6 SERVINGS

When is a shrimp cocktail not just a shrimp cocktail? When it has a shot of vodka in the sauce. Like many other dishes, this recipe is not an invention of the Sixties, but it seemed to reach its apogee during the era, perhaps as more people found middle-class affluence and dined out more often. For a wow factor, use the largest shrimp you can afford, at least 16 to 21 to a pound, or even larger.

BLOODY MARY COCKTAIL SAUCE

1¼ cups ketchup-style chili sauce
1 small celery rib with leaves, minced
1 tablespoon prepared horseradish
1 tablespoon fresh lemon juice
1 tablespoon finely chopped fresh parsley
1 tablespoon vodka
A few dashes of hot red pepper sauce

SHRIMP COCKTAIL

1 small onion, sliced
1 lemon, sliced
½ teaspoon salt
¼ teaspoon black peppercorns
1 bay leaf
30 jumbo or very large shrimp (about 1½ pounds), unpeeled

1. To make the cocktail sauce, combine all of the ingredients in a small bowl. Cover and refrigerate to blend the flavors, at least 2 hours or overnight.

2. Bring 1 quart water, with the onion, lemon, salt, peppercorns, and bay leaf to a boil in a large saucepan over high heat. Reduce the heat to low and simmer for 10 minutes. Add the shrimp and cook until they turn opaque and firm, 2 to 3 minutes. Drain and let cool. Peel and devein the shrimp. Cover and refrigerate until chilled, at least 1 hour. (The shrimp can be prepared up to 1 day ahead.)

3. For each serving, hook 5 shrimp in a circle around the edge of a martini glass, tails facing out. Spoon about ¼ cup of the sauce into the center of each glass. Serve chilled.

COCONUT SHRIMP WITH HOT CHINESE MUSTARD AND DUCK SAUCE

MAKES 6 TO 8 SERVINGS

Like crab Rangoon, there is only one way golden brown coconut shrimp can be made: deep-fried. In the Sixties, these would require a trip to a health food store or Chinatown to get unsweetened desiccated coconut; thankfully today, it's much more widely available. A word of warning: don't try to use sweetened flaked coconut as its sugary coating burns quickly in hot oil.

HOT CHINESE MUSTARD

½ cup mustard powder, such as Colman's
⅓ cup boiling water, as needed

COCONUT SHRIMP

1 cup all-purpose flour
1 teaspoon baking power
¼ teaspoon salt
1 large egg, beaten
1 cup club soda
Vegetable oil, for deep-frying
24 large shrimp, peeled and deveined
1¼ cups desiccated coconut
Duck Sauce, for dipping

1. To make the hot mustard, put mustard powder in a small bowl and whisk. Whisk in enough boiling water to give the desired consistency. Let stand, uncovered, for at least 1 hour before serving. (The mustard can be made up to 5 days ahead, refrigerated in a covered container.)

2. Whisk the flour, baking powder, salt, and egg together in a medium bowl. Whisk in the club soda. Let stand for 10 minutes.

3. Position a rack in the center of the oven and preheat the oven to 200°F. Line a baking sheet with waxed paper. Line a second baking sheet with a brown paper bag.

4. Pour enough oil into a deep, heavy saucepan to fill halfway up the sides. Heat over high heat to 350°F on a deep-frying thermometer.

5. Spread the coconut on a plate. One at a time, hold a shrimp by the tail and dip into the batter, letting the excess batter drip into the bowl. Roll the shrimp in the coconut to coat, and place on the waxed paper-lined baking sheet.

6. In batches without crowding, add the shrimp and deep-fry until golden brown, about 2½ minutes. Using a wire spider or a slotted spoon, transfer the shrimp to the brown paper-lined baking sheet and keep warm in the oven while frying the remaining shrimp.

7. Transfer to a serving platter and serve warm with the hot mustard and duck sauce.

Fearless Frying

Deep-frying is just that—frying food in a couple of inches of hot oil. You are not doing anyone any favors—you, the food, or your guests—by using less oil than required. Wimping out and cooking in a shallow pool of oil is a sure way of getting oily, soggy food. Be generous with the oil, and follow the tips below, and you will be rewarded with the crispy, crunchy stuff that is worth ruining your diet over.

- **Use a heavy pot with a capacity of at least 5 quarts.**
- **Don't save the used oil for another frying session. Let it cool, place in a covered container, and put in the garbage. (Unless you have a vegetable oil recycling station nearby.)**
- **Fill the pot with at least 1 quart of oil. Generic vegetable oil is reasonably priced and fine for deep-frying.**
- **Use a deep-frying thermometer to gauge the heat. Never let the temperature get about 400°F, the point where the oil will start to smoke and change flavor.**
- **A wide-meshed wire spider (available at kitchenware stores and online) is a great tool for removing the food from the oil because it encourages rapid drainage. A slotted spoon is an okay second choice.**
- **Brown paper bags are better for draining fried foods than paper towels.**

SPAM AND PINEAPPLE KEBABS

MAKES 32 KEBABS

You didn't think that we were going to skip Spam, did you? It was on practically every pantry shelf in the Sixties, ready to be turned into a quick meal. We fondly remember lunches of grilled Spam sandwiches, or as a special treat, an entire can studded with cloves and baked with mustard. Spam is beloved in Hawaii, where it gained popularity as an AP commodity, so it is only appropriate that it shows up on a pupu platter every now and then.

1 (12-ounce) can Spam, drained
1 (20-ounce) can pineapple chunks in heavy syrup
1 tablespoon soy sauce
32 small wooden skewers, soaked in water for 30 minutes, drained

1. Cut the Spam into 32 pieces about 1-inch square. Drain the pineapple and reserve 1 tablespoon of the syrup. Mix the syrup and soy sauce in a small bowl.

2. Skewer the 2 Spam pieces and 1 pineapple chunk on each skewer. (The kebabs can be prepared up to 12 hours ahead, covered and refrigerated.)

3. Position a broiler rack about 8 inches from the source of heat and preheat the broiler on High. Lightly oil the broiler rack.

4. Brush the Spam and pineapple lightly with the soy sauce mixture. Broil, turning occasionally, until lightly browned, about 3 minutes. Serve hot.

NOTE: If you have a hibachi with your pupu platter, the kebabs can be cooked directly over the heat source (usually Sterno).

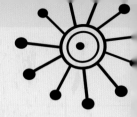

Mai Tai Madness

Light the tiki torches, mix up some crazy rum drinks, pass the
pupus, and try not to sacrifice anyone in a volcano. . . .

Mai Tais (page 190)

Blue Hawaiians (page 185)

Crab Rangoon (page 22)

Coconut Shrimp with Hot Chinese Mustard and Duck Sauce (page 43)

Rumaki-a-rama (page 39)

Spam and Pineapple Kebabs (page 45)

Macadamia nuts

Pineapple Upside-Down Cake (page 153)

Kona coffee

CD PLAYLIST

Ultra-Lounge, *Tiki Sampler*

Martin Denny, *The Exotic Sounds of Martin Denny*

Yma Sumac, *Voice of the Xtabay*

The Price of Milk . . . Inflated

Price tags were certainly lower in the Sixties than they are today, but was stuff really cheaper? Considering that $1 in 1963 had the same buying power as $7.10 in 2010, you might be surprised. Groceries were slightly more expensive back then, but we'd kill for those gas and house prices!

cost in 1963/cost in terms of 2010 inflation

Gallon of milk	$0.49	$2.79
Dozen eggs	$0.55	$1.37
Ground beef, per pound	$0.47	$3.78
Gallon of gas	$0.30	$2.73
Average price of a new home	$12,650	$268,700

Surprisingly Expensive

The modern age of electric appliances might have made life easier for a housewife, but they came at a pretty price!

cost in 1963/cost in terms of 2010 inflation

Automatic can opener	$8.88	$63.05
Vacuum cleaner	$59.99	$425.93
Dishwasher	$218.88	$1,554
26-inch color TV	$379	$2,691

EAT-BY-THE-BARREL TV MIX

MAKES ABOUT 15 SERVINGS

Kix and Cheerios both tried out "TV Mix" recipes, but the clear winner was Ralston Purina's Chex. Although the company, now owned by General Mills, has been printing the recipe for their "Chex Party Mix" on their cereal boxes since 1954, they only got around to patenting it in 1990. The recipe on their own website marked "the original" doesn't quite cut it for us, as we're fairly sure they didn't have bagel chips back then. Crunchy and salty, with a little sweetness from the breakfast cereal, this mix is impossible to stop eating.

6 tablespoons (¾ stick) unsalted butter, cut into tablespoons

3 tablespoons Worcestershire sauce

1 tablespoon hot red pepper sauce

1½ teaspoons seasoned salt

¾ teaspoon garlic powder

½ teaspoon onion powder

9 cups of crunchy breakfast cereal squares, such as Chex Brand Cereals (Corn, Rice, and/or Wheat), in any combination

1 (8-ounce) container salted mixed nuts

2 cups pretzel sticks or miniature pretzels

1. Preheat the oven to 250°F.

2. Melt the butter in a very large roasting pan over medium heat, stirring to be sure that the butter doesn't burn. Remove from the heat and stir in the Worcestershire sauce, hot red pepper sauce, seasoned salt, garlic powder, and onion powder. Gradually add the breakfast cereal, nuts, and pretzels, stirring well after each addition to coat the ingredients well.

3. Bake, stirring well every 15 minutes (this is important, or the mix will burn, so use a timer), until the mix is crisp and aromatic with garlicky-oniony scents, about 1 hour. Let cool completely. (The mix can be made up to 3 days ahead, stored in airtight containers at room temperature.)

KITCHEN TIME MACHINE

Substitute margarine for the butter, and omit the hot red pepper sauce. If you really want to recall the true original flavor, then the margarine is a must.

TV Highlights of 1963

- The FCC officially authorizes the remote control.
- Soap opera *General Hospital* premieres.
- *Leave It to Beaver* airs its final original episode.
- Six-year-old Donny Osmond makes his singing debut on *The Andy Williams Show.*
- The Los Angeles Dodgers (formerly the Brooklyn Dodgers) shut the New York Yankees out of the World Series.
- CBS expands its evening program from 15 to 30 minutes; NBC follows a week later.
- All three networks, ABC, CBS, and NBC, preempt programming to cover the Kennedy assassination.
- Jack Ruby kills Lee Harvey Oswald on live TV.

CHAPTER 3

VICHYSSOISE, ICEBERG, AND ASPIC . . . OH MY!
SOUPS, SALADS, AND SANDWICHES

Lunch, like the rest of the Sixties, was a mix of old and new. Comfort food, like grilled cheese sandwiches and chicken soup, was joined by the more upscale vichyssoise and artistic aspics. And in some cases, homegrown and gourmet were combined.

In the quest to make everyday food more sophisticated, many Sixties cooks took simple recipes and elaborated on them. Sandwiches were stacked into a "loaf" and cut at the table, revealing colorful layers. Instead of tossing torn crisphead lettuce with dressing, it was cut into a giant slice and drizzled with blue cheese and bacon, making perhaps the world's first deconstructed salad: the iceberg wedge.

TOMATO AND SHRIMP ASPIC

MAKES 8 TO 10 SERVINGS

This classic molded salad has a tomato and vegetable flavor reminiscent of gazpacho. As it must chill for a few hours, there is very little last-minute fussing. All you have to do is put down your vodka gimlet when unmolding it.

4 cups canned tomato juice; divided
3 envelopes unflavored powdered gelatin
1 small onion, thickly sliced
1 small celery rib with leaves, coarsely chopped, plus 2 tablespoons diced (¼-inch) celery
1 bay leaf
2 cups cooked cocktail (baby) shrimp
2 tablespoons seeded and (¼-inch) diced green bell pepper
2 tablespoons finely chopped pimiento-stuffed green olives
Salt
Hot red pepper sauce
Vegetable oil, for the ring mold
Salad greens, for serving

1. Pour 1 cup of the tomato juice in a small bowl. Sprinkle the gelatin on top and let stand while heating the tomato juice, stirring the mixture a few times so the gelatin is completely moistened.

2. Combine the remaining 3 cups tomato juice with the onion, the coarsely chopped celery rib, and the bay leaf in a nonreactive medium saucepan. Bring to a simmer over medium heat. Reduce the heat to very low and heat at a bare simmer for 15 minutes. Remove from the heat and add the soaked gelatin mixture. Stir with a rubber spatula, scraping down the sides of the saucepan often, until the gelatin is completely dissolved, about 2 minutes.

3. Strain the tomato juice mixture through a wire sieve into a heatproof medium bowl. Discard the solids in the sieve. Place the bowl in a larger bowl of icy water. Let stand, stirring occasionally, until the tomato juice mixture is cool and thickened to the consistency of very soft pudding, about 30 minutes. (You can skip the icy water and simply refrigerate the tomato juice in its bowl until partially set, but it will take about 1½ hours.) Fold in the shrimp, diced celery and green pepper, and olives. Season with the salt and hot red pepper sauce.

4. Pour into a lightly oiled 6-cup ring mold. Cover with plastic wrap and refrigerate until set, at least 4 hours or overnight.

5. To unmold, run a dinner knife around the inside of the mold. Dip the mold in a large bowl or sink of warm water for 5 seconds. Dry the outside of the mold with a kitchen towel. Invert onto a serving platter. Hold the mold and platter together and give them a sharp shake or two to unmold the salad onto the platter. Slice and serve chilled on a bed of salad greens.

Watch It Wiggle

Now known mainly as a fruity dessert medium, gelatin began as a carnivore's friend. In the days before refrigeration, as far back as the Middle Ages, gelatin was used to help preserve cooked meat as it provided a barrier to air and bacteria. Originally gelatin took the form of an unflavored jelly that was spread over food, but in the eighteenth century, it was refined to the consistency we know today. Instead of just a coating, gelatin became a main ingredient as cooks experimented with color, flavor, and clarity. Savory food suspended in gelatin became known as aspic, possibly after the Greek word for "shield," *aspis*. When powdered Knox gelatin became common in the late nineteenth century, aspics became the last word in stylish dining.

This trend was still in full-force in the Sixties, and every serious cook's kitchen sported a gelatin mold, often made of copper and proudly displayed from a nail on the kitchen walls. Limited only by the imagination, aspics became culinary showcases of color and creativity.

ICEBERG LETTUCE WEDGE WITH BLUE CHEESE DRESSING AND BACON

MAKES 4 SERVINGS

An iceberg wedge is sturdy, to say the least, and is best when served with a full-bodied dressing that cling to its curves, like this homemade blue cheese. When you are feeling flush, use a fine imported blue cheese; otherwise, Danish blue is just fine. Don't feel like blue cheese dressing? We've added our favorite salad dressings as options, all perfect for smothering an iceberg chunk.

BLUE CHEESE DRESSING

⅔ cup mayonnaise
⅔ cup sour cream
½ cup buttermilk
6 ounces (1¼ cups) crumbled blue cheese, such as Roquefort, Gorgonzola, or Danish blue
Salt and freshly ground black pepper

8 slices bacon
1 head iceberg lettuce, quartered lengthwise into wedges, rinsed well, and patted dry

1. To make the dressing, whisk the mayonnaise, sour cream, and buttermilk together in a medium bowl. Add the blue cheese and mix with a rubber spatula, mashing some of the cheese into the dressing. Season with salt and pepper. Cover and refrigerate until chilled, at least 1 hour and up to 3 days.

2. Position a rack in the center of the oven and preheat to 400°F. Arrange the bacon on a rimmed baking sheet. Bake until crisp and golden brown, about 20 minutes. Transfer the bacon to paper towels. Reserve the bacon fat for another use (see page 35). Let the bacon cool, then coarsely chop.

3. To serve, stand an iceberg wedge on a dinner plate. Divide the dressing over each wedge, then sprinkle with equal amounts of the bacon. Serve chilled.

RED FRENCH DRESSING: Process ¼ cup ketchup, 2 tablespoons cider vinegar, 2 tablespoons chopped shallot or red onion, 1½ teaspoons light or dark brown sugar, ½ teaspoon dry mustard, 1 minced garlic clove, ¼ teaspoon salt, and ⅛ teaspoon freshly ground black pepper in a blender. With the machine running, gradually pour ⅔ cup vegetable oil through a vent in the lid.

GREEN GODDESS DRESSING: Whisk together 2 tablespoons fresh lemon juice and 1½ teaspoons anchovy paste in a bowl to dissolve the anchovy paste. Add 1 cup mayonnaise, ½ cup sour cream, 1 large minced scallion (white and green parts), 2 tablespoons minced fresh parsley, and 1 tablespoon minced fresh tarragon. Season with salt and pepper.

THOUSAND ISLAND DRESSING: Whisk together 1 cup mayonnaise, ⅓ cup ketchup-style chili sauce, 3 tablespoons sweet pickle relish, 1 minced scallion (white and green parts), 2 tablespoons drained and rinsed capers (preferably nonpareil, and chopped if standard large capers), and 2 tablespoons minced pimiento-stuffed olives. Season with hot red pepper sauce.

Lettuce Rejoice

Even though it's ridiculed by modern foodies as the "polyester of lettuce," iceberg lettuce was a miracle to midcentury diners.

Before its "invention" in the 1930s, lettuce could only be enjoyed when it was harvested fresh from local growers since it can't be canned, frozen, or dried to any real satisfaction. And once it's picked, it begins to wilt quickly. Farmers in California discovered that the cabbage-shaped crisphead lettuce, when packed in ice, could be transported in special cooling containers year round. Crisphead was rechristened iceberg, and became a salvation to salad lovers.

Iceberg lettuce was hugely popular in the Sixties, and continues to dominate the market in America even in the present day. It was favored by dieters for its juicy bulk, and adored by the masses for its crunch as it offered a cool, crispy addition to soft sandwiches and squishy veggies.

WALDORF SALAD

Created by the maître d'hôtel at the Hotel Waldorf, the first hotel in the world to offer room service, Waldorf salad can be a candy-sweet combination of fresh apples, celery, and lettuce tossed in mayonnaise. Although not part of the original recipe, walnuts are now considered a classic inclusion. Two tricks make this version extra special: toasting the nuts, and adding a little sour cream and poppy seeds to the dressing.

1 cup walnut pieces
½ cup mayonnaise
2 tablespoons sour cream
1 tablespoon poppy seeds
4 Red Delicious or other sweet red apples, cored and cut into ½-inch dice
4 large celery ribs, cut into ½-inch slices
Salt
Freshly ground black pepper
Green lettuce leaves, for serving

1. Position a rack in the center of the oven and preheat the oven to 350°F. Spread the walnuts on a baking sheet. Bake, stirring occasionally, until the walnuts are toasted and fragrant, about 10 minutes. Let cool completely.

2. Whisk the mayonnaise, sour cream, and poppy seeds together in a medium bowl. Add the toasted nuts with the apples and celery and fold together until combined. Season with salt and pepper. Cover and refrigerate until chilled, at least 1 and up to 4 hours. (The acidity of the dressing will keep the apples from discoloring.)

3. Arrange the lettuce in a serving bowl and heap the apple mixture in the center of the bowl. Serve chilled.

KITCHEN TIME MACHINE

To make this a more substantial main course salad, add 2 cups cooked and cubed chicken and 1 additional tablespoon each of mayonnaise and sour cream. In the Sixties, you would have had to cook the chicken yourself (see Chicken Divan, page 102), but supermarket rotisserie chicken works perfectly.

MANHATTAN CLAM CHOWDER

Manhattan clam chowder differs from its New England namesake in that it has a tomato base instead of cream. A healthy soup chunky with vegetables and a tomato-y tang suitable for dieters, it's also a very democratic soup. You might find it listed both as the "soup du jour" on the menu blackboard at the neighborhood bar and grill, and as a specialty of the house at tony seafood palaces. Homemade is best.

2 large baking potatoes, peeled and cut into ½-inch dice
4 bacon slices, coarsely chopped
1 medium onion, chopped
3 medium celery ribs with leaves, cut into ½-inch dice
1 medium carrot, cut into ½-inch dice
½ cup (½-inch) seeded and diced green bell pepper
3 cups bottled clam juice
1 (28-ounce) can whole tomatoes in juice, juices reserved, chopped (see Note)
½ teaspoon dried thyme
1 bay leaf
1 (1-pound) container shucked clams with juice
Salt and freshly ground black pepper
Chopped fresh parsley, for garnish

1. Bring a medium saucepan of salted water to a boil over high heat. Add the potatoes and return to a boil. Reduce the heat to medium and partially cover the saucepan. Simmer until the potatoes are barely tender, 10 to 15 minutes. Drain and set aside.

2. Meanwhile, cook the bacon in a large saucepan over medium heat, stirring occasionally, until crisp and browned, about 8 minutes. Using a slotted spoon, transfer the bacon to paper towels to drain.

3. Add the onion, celery, carrot, and green pepper to the fat in the saucepan. Cover and cook, stirring occasionally, until softened, about 3 minutes. Add the clam juice, tomatoes with their juice, thyme, and bay leaf and stir well. Bring to a boil over high heat. Reduce the heat to medium-low and partially cover the saucepan. Simmer to blend the flavors, about 25 minutes.

4. Stir in the clams and their juices with the bacon and potatoes. Cook just to heat the clams and potatoes, about 3 minutes. Season with salt and pepper.

5. Ladle into bowls and serve hot, sprinkled with parsley.

NOTE: Here's a low-tech way to chop tomatoes. Pour the contents of the can into a deep bowl. Reach into the bowl and crush the tomatoes through your impeccably clean fingers until the tomatoes are broken into pieces about the size of a quarter or smaller. That's it.

BLENDER GAZPACHO

In the Sixties, the cold Spanish soup was all the rage with the fashionable crowd in Manhattan. It was exotic, refreshing, and seasonally delicious. To streamline the chore of chopping so many vegetables, even Spanish cooks used a blender.

3 large ripe tomatoes
1 large cucumber, peeled
1 medium green bell pepper, seeded and diced
1 medium yellow onion, coarsely chopped
2 garlic cloves, finely chopped
2 tablespoons olive oil, preferably extra-virgin
1 tablespoon red wine vinegar
2 cups canned tomato juice, preferably tomato-vegetable juice
Salt and freshly ground black pepper
Chopped tomatoes, cucumbers, and green bell peppers and croutons, for toppings

1. Cut the tomatoes in half through their equators, and gently squeeze to remove the seeds. Slice the cucumber lengthwise and scoop out and discard the seeds with the dip of a spoon. Coarsely chop the tomatoes and cucumber.

2. In batches, puree the tomatoes, cucumber, green pepper, onion, garlic, oil, and vinegar together with the tomato juice. Transfer to a bowl. Season with salt and pepper. Cover and refrigerate until chilled, at least 2 hours or overnight.

3. Place the tomatoes, cucumber, green peppers, and croutons in individual serving bowls. Ladle the soup into soup bowls and serve chilled, letting each guest add toppings from the serving bowls as desired.

VICHYSSOISE

Here's another popular cold soup from the period, this one French in name but American in origin. Vichyssoise (pronounced VEE-shee-swahz, with a hard "z" on the end) was invented by Louis Diat, the chef at the Ritz-Carlton in Manhattan. He recalled cooling a potato and leek soup with cold cream during the summer when he was growing up, and named the soup for the French town of Vichy. It's a perfect soup for the cool host or hostess because it must be cooked well ahead of serving, leaving you less to stress about on party day.

4 large leeks
1 medium onion, chopped
2 tablespoons vegetable oil
5 cups canned reduced-sodium chicken broth
1½ pounds baking potatoes, such as russet or Burbank, peeled and cubed
½ cup heavy cream
Salt and freshly ground white pepper
Sour cream, for serving
Finely chopped fresh chives, for garnish

1. Chop the white and pale green parts of the leeks, discarding the green tops. You should have 3 packed cups of chopped leeks. Transfer the leeks to a bowl of large water and agitate them in the water to dislodge any grit. Let stand for a few minutes, letting the grit sink to the bottom of the bowl. Lift the leeks from the water, leaving the grit behind. Spin the leeks in a salad spinner to remove excess water.

2. Heat the oil in a soup pot over medium heat. Add the leeks and onion and cover. Cook, stirring occasionally, until softened, about 5 minutes. Add the broth and potatoes and bring to a boil over high heat. Reduce the heat to medium-low and partially cover the pot with the lid. Simmer until the potatoes are tender, about 25 minutes.

3. In batches, with the lid ajar to avoid a geyser of hot soup, puree the soup in a blender, transferring the puree to a bowl. Stir in the cream, then season with salt and pepper. Let cool until tepid. Cover and refrigerate until chilled, at least 3 hours or overnight.

4. Just before serving, taste and adjust the seasoning with salt and pepper. Ladle into soup bowls. Top each serving with a dollop of sour cream and a sprinkle of chives and serve chilled.

SIXTIES SECRET GRILLED CHEESE SANDWICH

MAKES 4 SANDWICHES

Think grilled cheese sandwiches are the same now as they were in the Sixties? Not according to our source, the former grill cook at a popular midcentury diner. They used white bread and American cheese, but shunned butter for a not-so-secret Sixties ingredient: mayonnaise.

4 slices white sandwich bread
8 slices American cheese
About 2 tablespoons mayonnaise

1. Using 2 slices of bread and 2 slices of American cheese for each sandwich, make 4 sandwiches. Spread a thin schmear of mayonnaise on the outsides of the sandwiches.

2. Heat a large griddle or two heavy skillets over medium heat. Place the sandwiches on the griddle and adjust the heat to medium-low. Cook until the underside is golden brown, about 2 minutes, adjusting the heat as needed so the sandwich doesn't cook and brown too rapidly. Turn and cook until the other side is golden brown, about 2 minutes longer. Transfer to plates, cut in half on the diagonal, and serve hot.

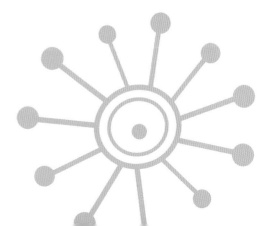

CREAM OF TOMATO SOUP

As pop artist Andy Warhol's 1962 painting *100 Soup Cans* affirms, the early Sixties was the age of canned soup. Campbell's first ready-to-serve soup flavor was tomato, and it remains one of its three most popular soups to this day. While cracking open a can is perfectly acceptable when you're alone, it's hardly a way to treat company. Try this simple, homemade tomato soup recipe (especially with our Sixties Secret Grilled Cheese Sandwich, page 61), and you might just retire your can opener.

2 tablespoons unsalted butter
1 medium onion, chopped
1 medium celery rib, chopped
2 tablespoons all-purpose flour
3 cups canned reduced-sodium chicken broth
1 (28-ounce) can whole tomatoes in juice, juices reserved, chopped (see Note, page 57)
1 bay leaf
⅓ cup heavy cream
Salt and freshly ground black pepper

1. Melt the butter in a large saucepan over medium heat. Add the onion and celery and cover. Cook, stirring occasionally, until softened, about 5 minutes. Sprinkle in the flour and stir well. Add the broth, the tomatoes and their juices, and the bay leaf. Bring to a simmer. Reduce the heat to medium-low and simmer, partially covered, until the celery is very tender, about 20 minutes. Remove the bay leaf.

2. In batches, transfer the soup to a blender and puree. Return to the saucepan and stir in the cream. Reheat, but do not boil. Season with salt and pepper. Serve hot.

Mmm, Mmm . . . Art

Andy Warhol's original *Campbell's Soup Cans* was a work of art consisting of thirty-two individual 20-by-16-inch canvases each displaying a realistic painting of each of the varieties of soup Campbell's sold in the early Sixties. Its premiere in 1962 marked Warhol's first one-man gallery debut, the introduction of pop art to the West Coast, and a sea of outrage from the art world, which dismissed it as vulgar and common. The controversy solidified Warhol's celebrity.

But why soup cans? Was it a deliberate nod to the "nothingness" movement of the time? A crass embrace of commercialism from the man who correctly predicted: "In the future, everyone will be world-famous for 15 minutes"? Or maybe it was just as his fellow pop artist and friend Robert Indiana believed, "The reason he painted soup cans is that he liked soup."

The wily artist famously known for repeatedly changing stories about himself to confuse interviewers never gave a single answer. He admitted he did like Campbell's soup, claimed to have drank a can a day for lunch for twenty years, and stated it was a random choice, just something he saw every day.

However, chefs-turned-psychologists that we are, we think we've discovered the answer: it was because of his mother. In 1985, Warhol told an interviewer from London's *Face* magazine that his mother used to cut tin flowers out of soup and fruit cans and sell them for extra money concluding, "that's the reason why I did my first tin-can paintings."

True or not, since Campbell's boasted four out of every five cans of soup sold in the U.S. during Warhol's childhood, and he admitted a penchant for the tomato variety especially, we think his early culinary experiences and watching his crafty mother shaped his subconscious. Good Food + Loving Mama = Art. We knew it.

DATE NUT BREAD AND CREAM CHEESE SANDWICHES

. . . .
MAKES 8 SERVINGS
. . . .

With the natural sweetness of dates in every bite, date nut bread is a sneaky way to get kids to eat fruit without their knowing it. These dainty sandwiches were considered very classy fare, and all of the best luncheon places served them. If you don't want to make a sandwich, you can just cut a slab off the loaf and eat it with a cold glass of milk . . . or an Old-Fashioned. We won't tell your kids.

1½ cups pitted and chopped dates (see Note on page 66)
4 tablespoons (½ stick) unsalted butter, plus room temperature butter for the pan
¾ cup packed light brown sugar
2 large eggs
1 teaspoon vanilla extract
1½ cups all-purpose flour, plus more for the pan
1½ teaspoons baking powder
½ teaspoon ground cinnamon
½ teaspoon ground nutmeg
½ teaspoon salt
¼ teaspoon baking soda
1 cup coarsely chopped walnuts
4 ounces cream cheese, softened

---

1. Position a rack in the center of the oven and preheat the oven to 350°F. Lightly butter an 8 ½-by-4 ½-inch loaf pan. Line the bottom of the pan with waxed paper. Dust the inside of the pan with flour and tap out the excess.

2. Bring ¾ cup water, the dates, and butter to a boil in a small saucepan over medium heat. Pour into a medium bowl. Let stand, stirring often, until tepid, about 30 minutes. Transfer about ½ cup of the date mixture (including the soaking liquid) to a blender and process into a puree, adding more of the soaking liquid as needed. Stir the puree into the remaining date mixture. Add the brown sugar, eggs, and vanilla and whisk well.

3. Sift the flour, baking powder, cinnamon, nutmeg, salt, and baking soda together into a medium bowl. Make a well in the dry ingredients, pour in the date mixture, and stir with a spoon just until combined. Fold in the walnuts. Scrape into the prepared pan and smooth the top.

4. Bake until a wooden skewer inserted into the center of the loaf comes out without any clinging batter, about 55 minutes. Transfer to a wire cake rack and let cool for 10 minutes. Unmold onto the rack, remove the waxed paper, and turn right side up. Let cool completely.

5. Cut the loaf into 10 slices. Cut each slice in half crosswise. Spread a pair of halves with cream cheese and sandwich them together. (The sandwiches can be wrapped in plastic wrap and refrigerated for up to 1 day. Let stand at room temperature for 1 hour before serving.) Serve at room temperature.

NOTE: For convenience, buy chopped dates. If you prefer to chop them yourself, use oiled scissors to snip them into ½ inch or smaller pieces. Do not try to do the job with a blender or food processor, or you will end with a gummy ball of dates.

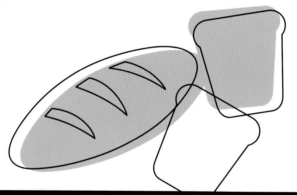

Ground Beef by Any Other Name . . .

Sloppy Joes might have more regional nicknames than any other food. In the Midwest they're called Yip Yips or Yum Yums. Other monikers include Dynamites, Slushburgers, Steamers, Taverns, Wimpies, and Hot Tamales. Our all time favorite name? Manwich, the brand name of canned Sloppy Joe introduced by Hunt's in 1969. However, in northern New Jersey, a Sloppy Joe is something else entirely—a triple decker sandwich with sliced meat, coleslaw, and Russian dressing.

SLOPPY JOES

A staple of the Sixties school lunchroom, Sloppy Joes are messy, but satisfying. If you've only ever eaten it from the can, your mom is younger than our moms. Do yourself a favor and make it from scratch.

1 tablespoon vegetable oil
1 medium yellow onion, chopped
1 medium celery rib, chopped
½ small green bell pepper, seeded and chopped
1¾ pounds ground round (85% lean)
1 (8-ounce) can tomato sauce
½ cup tomato ketchup
1 tablespoon Worcestershire sauce
1 tablespoon prepared yellow mustard
1 tablespoon cider vinegar
1 tablespoon light brown sugar
Salt and freshly ground black pepper
6 hamburger buns, toasted

1. Heat the oil in a large skillet over medium heat. Add the onion, celery, and green pepper and cook, stirring often, until softened, about 5 minutes. Add the ground round and cook, stirring occasionally, breaking up the meat with the side of the spoon, until the meat loses its raw look, about 10 minutes. Drain off the fat in the skillet.

2. Stir in the tomato sauce, ketchup, Worcestershire sauce, mustard, vinegar, and brown sugar and bring to a simmer. Reduce the heat to medium-low and simmer, stirring occasionally, until the sauce has thickened, about 20 minutes.

3. Divide the mixture evenly among the buns and serve hot.

Housewife Helper

Technology in the post-war, space-age 1940s and '50s gave birth to the convenience foods craze. Foods that were notoriously difficult to make from scratch were now offered prepared and prepackaged. What began as an offering of single items like orange juice concentrate and quick-cooking rice morphed into a whole menu of ready-made foods.

Some were instant hits—frozen fish sticks and tubs of frosting—while some never quite took off—cheeseburger in a can, anyone? The rise of convenience food meant an increase in the personal fortunes of places like the fictional Sterling Cooper ad agency on *Mad Men*, as manufacturers threw big bucks at Madison Avenue. Introducing new products that changed the way people had been thinking about food for hundreds of years required a lot of creative advertising. How else to explain that by adding water to little white flakes, you could get instant mashed potatoes? Until Reddi-wip, the only thing squirting out of an aerosol can was insecticide (even shaving cream came later).

The processed food revolution was sponsored, sung about, and of course, televised. While product-centri cookbooks and inventive new recipes (usually distributed to the public for free) were still used, broadcasting demanded more than just words. Slogans, jingles, and even dances were invented to schlep product.

To sell their canned barbecue sauce and beef in the Sixties, Libby's created a commercial to introduce "a brand new dance" called the Sloppy Joe. Teenagers took bites of imaginary sandwiches and then rubbed their tummies to the tune of "just heat, and eat, and swing to the beat!" It's a little piece of advertising gold well worth looking up on YouTube. (We want to know where we can get those nifty sweatshirts that say "Beef"—yes, in actual quotes—and "Pork.")

STACKED SALMON AND EGG SALAD SANDWICH

• • • • • • • •
MAKES 8 SERVINGS
• • • • • • • •

In the world of Sixties social status, sometimes adversaries had to be taken out over food. Did the neighborhood hussy, we mean *divorcée*, hit on your husband? Caught someone cheating in bridge club? Rather than freak out (or flip a table), a gentler way to defeat your foes is to showcase your superior culinary skills. Bring this frosted treat to the table, cut into it and—*bam!*—reveal its layers of pretty pink-and-yellow layers. Checkmate.

SALMON SALAD

    1 pound salmon fillet with skin
    Salt
    Freshly ground black pepper
    2 tablespoons mayonnaise
    1 small celery rib, minced
    Hot red pepper sauce

EGG SALAD

    3 hard-boiled eggs (see page 24), peeled and finely chopped
    2 tablespoons mayonnaise
    3 tablespoons minced scallion, white and green parts
    Salt
    Freshly ground black pepper

    1 unsliced loaf white bread (about 1¼ pounds)
    12 ounces cream cheese, at room temperature
    ½ cup mayonnaise
    1 tablespoon fresh lemon juice
    Fresh watercress sprigs, canned pimiento slices, and sliced green or black olives, for garnish

1. To make the salmon salad, position a rack in the center of the oven and preheat to 400°F. Lightly oil a baking sheet. Place the salmon on the baking sheet, skin side down. Season with ¼ teaspoon salt and ¼ teaspoon pepper. Bake until the salmon looks opaque when flaked in the center with the tip of a knife, about 20 minutes. Let cool completely.

2. Flake the salmon, discarding the skin, and place the salmon meat in a medium bowl. Add the mayonnaise and celery and mix. Season with salt and hot red pepper sauce.

3. To make the egg salad, mix the eggs, mayonnaise, and scallion in a medium bowl. Season with salt and pepper.

4. Slice the bread horizontally into 4 equal layers. Place the first bread layer on a large sheet of plastic wrap. Spread with half of the salmon salad. Top with the following bread layer, then spread with the egg salad. Add the next layer of bread, the remaining salmon salad, and the final top bread layer. Tightly wrap the stacked layers in plastic wrap, using more wrap as needed. Refrigerate for at least 1 hour or overnight.

5. Mix the cream cheese, mayonnaise, and lemon juice together in a medium bowl using an electric mixer on high speed until smooth. Unwrap the stacked bread. Use a metal icing spatula to spread the cream cheese mixture smoothly and evenly over the top and sides of the bread. Decorate the top with watercress, pimiento, and olives. Using a wide spatula, transfer to a serving platter. Refrigerate, uncovered, for at least 1 and up to 4 hours.

6. Cut into ¾-inch-thick slices and transfer to dinner plates. Serve chilled.

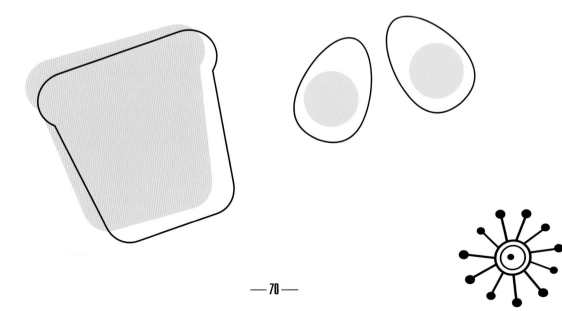

CHAPTER 4
COMPANY FOOD: MAIN COURSES

While everyone is quick to remember the Sixties for its convenience food and canned everything, the decade also ushered in America's modern gourmet renaissance. The woman who first brought French cooking into housewives' hearts before a single Julia Child book was published? Fashion and food icon Jacqueline Kennedy.

UNCOMMONLY DELICIOUS

Not all of the main courses served in the Sixties were gourmet of course, but they were, at least those served to "company," downright delicious. We'll take you step-by-step on our own "little trip around the world" with entrées from Sweden to Puerto Rico, from Staten Island to Malibu. We've got beef, pork, pasta, poultry, seafood, and even vegetarian. You don't have to be a Jackie or a Julia to whip up a midcentury feast. Cross our hearts.

Camelot in the Kitchen

Although political pundits thought women would hate the upper-class debutante, Jackie Kennedy was wildly popular. Women across the country looked to her as a beacon of continental sophistication. They dressed like her, styled their hair like her, and hoped to entertain like her.

Kennedy made big news when she brought a private chef with her to the White House—the first time since Thomas Jefferson that caterers and housekeepers wouldn't be in charge of state dinners. After interviewing him in French, Kennedy hired Paris-trained René Verdon. Where previously international cuisine had been thought of as unpatriotic, it was suddenly *en vogue.* His menus were enthusiastically reported by the press; his White House debut, a lunch for then-British Prime Minister Harold Macmillan, even made the front page of the *New York Times.*

One of the first chefs to embrace fresh, locally grown produce, Verdon planted vegetables on the White House roof and snuck herbs into the East Garden. He quit in a "Gallic huff" according to *Time* magazine when new President Lyndon Johnson insisted the White House kitchen use frozen vegetables. He was the author of five cookbooks and proprietor of several successful restaurants, including Le Trianon in San Francisco, where Rick enjoyed many a *soupe a l'oignon* in his college years.

BEEF WELLINGTON

It is possible that beef Wellington was named for the English duke who defeated Napoleon at the Battle of Waterloo, this has long been one of the most eye-popping main courses a cook can present to guests. As home cooks found their inner gourmet in the Sixties, beef Wellington became "the" dish. Original recipes called for homemade dough, but that's because frozen puff pastry wasn't mass-marketed until 1971. In a recipe this elaborate, why fight progress? If you're a purist and want to go for all from-scratch, make a double batch of the Perfect Pie Dough on page 163, and roll it out into a $1/8$-inch-thick rectangle large enough to wrap the beef, reserving any trimmings for decorating the pastry.

MADEIRA SAUCE

2 tablespoons unsalted butter
3 tablespoons minced onion
2 tablespoons all-purpose flour
2 cups canned reduced-sodium beef broth
½ cup Madeira (California Madeira is fine)
2 teaspoons tomato paste
¼ teaspoon dried thyme
½ bay leaf
Salt and freshly ground black pepper

BEEF

1 teaspoon dried thyme
1 teaspoon salt
½ teaspoon freshly ground black pepper
1 (3-pound) beef tenderloin, trimmed and tied
1 tablespoon vegetable oil

MUSHROOM DUXELLES

1½ pounds white mushrooms, finely chopped
2 tablespoons unsalted butter
½ cup chopped scallions, white parts only, or ¼ cup chopped shallots
1 garlic clove, minced
Salt and freshly ground black pepper

ASSEMBLY

All-purpose flour, for rolling out the dough
1 (17.3-ounce) package thawed frozen puff pastry sheets
4 ounces thinly sliced (but not paper-thin) prosciutto
6 ounces refrigerated or canned liver pâté or mousse, cut into ¼-inch-thick slices
1 large egg, beaten well

1. To make the sauce, melt the butter in a medium saucepan over medium heat. Add the onion and cook, stirring occasionally, until softened, about 3 minutes. Sprinkle with the flour and stir well. Whisk in the broth, Madeira, tomato paste, thyme, and bay leaf. Bring to a simmer, whisking often. Reduce the heat to medium-low. Simmer, stirring often, until the sauce has reduced to about 2 cups, about 35 minutes. Season with salt and pepper. Remove from the heat and set aside. (The sauce can be made, cooled, covered, and refrigerated, up to 2 days ahead.)

2. To prepare the beef, mix the thyme, salt, and pepper together in a small bowl. Rub all over the beef. Heat the oil in a very large skillet over medium-high heat. Add the beef and cook, turning occasionally, until nicely browned on all sides, about 10 minutes. Transfer to a rimmed baking sheet and let cool completely, about 1 hour.

3. Pour off the fat from the pan. Return the pan to medium-high heat and add ½ cup water. Cook, stirring up the browned bits in the pan with a wooden spoon, and boil until reduced to a glaze, about 1 minute. Stir into the Madeira sauce, and the juices will deepen the color of the sauce. (If the sauce seems too thin, simmer it for a few minutes to reduce it.)

4. To make the duxelles, very finely chop the mushrooms. (Or, in batches, pulse the mushrooms in a food processor fitted with the metal chopping blade until very finely chopped.) Melt the butter in a large skillet over medium heat. Add the mushrooms, scallions, and garlic and cook, stirring often, until the mushrooms give off their liquid and begin to brown, about 15 minutes. The mixture should resemble a spreadable paste. Season with salt and pepper. Transfer to a bowl and let cool completely.

5. To assemble the beef Wellington, be sure that the beef and duxelles are completely cooled. Lightly flour a work surface. Place the pastry sheets in front of you, overlapping them slightly. Dust the top of the pastry with flour and roll out into a 19-by-12-inch rectangle. Arrange half of the prosciutto, overlapping as needed, down the center of the pastry the same length and width as the beef. Top with half of the pâté, then half of the duxelles. Place the beef on top of the layered ingredients. Drape the remaining prosciutto over the top and sides of the beef. Place the remaining pâté on the beef, then press the remaining duxelles over the top and sides of the beef. It should be moist enough to stick, but if it falls off, don't worry. Use a pizza wheel or sharp knife to trim 1 inch from the perimeter of the pastry, and refrigerate the trimmings. Fold the pastry over the beef to enclose it into a packet, and seal the seams closed with some of the beaten egg. Transfer the pastry-wrapped beef, seam side down, onto an ungreased large rimmed baking sheet. Loosely cover with plastic wrap. Refrigerate, with the beaten egg, for at least 1 and up to 4 hours.

6. Position a rack in the center of the oven and preheat the oven to 425°F. Cut the reserved pastry trimmings into decorative shapes. (You can use small cookie or miniature aspic cutters, or even the end of a plain round pastry tip to make rounds.) Brush the pastry-wrapped beef all over with some of the beaten egg, and decorate with the pastry shapes. Brush again lightly with the beaten egg.

7. Bake for 10 minutes. Reduce the oven temperature to 375°F and continue baking until the pastry is golden brown and an instant-read thermometer inserted in the center of the beef (poke right through the crust) reads 125°F for medium-rare beef. Let stand for 10 minutes.

8. Meanwhile, reheat the sauce in a medium saucepan over medium heat until simmering. Season with salt and pepper. Strain through a sieve into a sauceboat or serving bowl.

9. Transfer the beef Wellington to a large oblong platter. Cut into ¾-inch-thick slices, and serve on dinner plates, with the sauce.

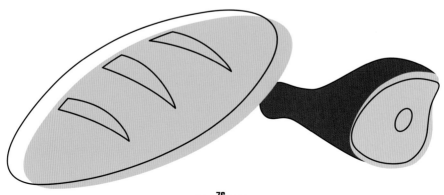

HUNGARIAN GOULASH GABOR

MAKES 6 SERVINGS

With the interest in European cooking dovetailing with air travel, Sixties cooks began learning how to made authentic versions of Americanized dishes. While goulash had previously been known as regular beef stew with paprika thrown in, the traditional recipe finally got its delicious due. (We couldn't help naming this after those Hungarian treats, Eva and Zsa Zsa Gabor, who were workhorses on Sixties television.) To discourage scorching on the stove, try baking it, as the heat will surround the pot rather than just concentrating on the bottom.

4 tablespoons bacon fat or vegetable oil, as needed
3 pounds beef chuck, cut into 1½-inch cubes
Salt and freshly ground black pepper
3 medium yellow onions, chopped
3 medium green bell peppers, seeded and chopped
3 garlic cloves, minced
¼ cup all-purpose flour
¼ cup sweet Hungarian paprika
4 cups canned reduced-sodium beef broth
Hot cooked noodles, for serving
Sour cream, for serving

1. Position a rack in the center of the oven and preheat the oven to 350°F.

2. Melt 2 tablespoons of bacon fat in a Dutch oven or flameproof casserole over medium-high heat. Season the beef with 1½ teaspoons salt and 1 teaspoon pepper. In batches, adding more fat as needed, add the beef and cook, turning occasionally, until browned, about 6 minutes. Transfer the beef to a plate.

3. Melt the remaining 2 tablespoons bacon fat in the Dutch oven over medium heat. Add the onions, bell pepper, and garlic and cover. Cook, stirring occasionally, until softened, about 6 minutes. Add the flour and paprika and stir well. Stir in the broth. Return the beef to the Dutch oven and bring to a simmer, stirring occasionally. Cover the Dutch oven.

4. Bake, stirring every 30 minutes, until the beef is very tender, about 1¾ hours. Season with salt and pepper. Serve hot, on the noodles, topping each serving with a dollop of sour cream.

COLD WAR BEEF STROGANOFF

MAKES 4 TO 6 SERVINGS

The American political situation with Russia didn't stop American moms from cooking up Russian food like blini, strawberries Romanoff, and beef Stroganoff. Many households made their Stroganoff with canned mushroom soup, but just as many made it from scratch. In either case, it scored big with busy cooks because it's ready to serve in no time. Even gourmets embraced Stroganoff, as it prominently featured mushrooms, which were about as exotic as one got (vegetable-wise) in the Cold War era.

1½ pounds boneless top loin (shell or New York) or sirloin steak
Salt and freshly ground black pepper
2 tablespoons vegetable oil
1 small onion, chopped
2 tablespoons unsalted butter
12 ounces white mushrooms, sliced
1¼ cups sour cream
1 teaspoon cornstarch
Chopped fresh parsley or chives, for garnish
Hot cooked noodles, for serving

1. Cut the steak across the grain into ½-inch-thick slices, trimming and discarding excess fat. Cut each slice into pieces 2 to 3 inches long. Season with ½ teaspoon salt and ¼ teaspoon pepper.

2. Heat the oil in a large skillet over medium-high heat. In batches without crowding, add the beef and cook, stirring often, until seared, about 3 minutes. The beef should be rare at this point.

3. Reduce the heat to medium. Add the onion and butter together to the skillet (don't add the butter alone, or it could burn from the retained heat) and cook, stirring often, until the onion softens, about 3 minutes. Add the mushrooms and cook, stirring occasionally, until their juices evaporate and the mushrooms begin to brown, about 10 minutes. Add ⅓ cup water to the skillet and bring to a boil, scraping up the browned bits in the skillet.

4. Return the beef to the skillet. Add the sour cream mixture and cook, stirring often, until the sauce comes to a simmer. (The cornstarch will keep the sour cream from curdling.) Season with salt and pepper. Sprinkle with the parsley. Serve hot, with the noodles.

PAN-FRIED STEAK WITH BUTTER

· · · · · · ·
MAKES 2 SERVINGS
· · · · · · ·

While backyard barbecues were popular in the suburbs, for most people, especially city dwellers, a steak at home meant taking out the cast-iron skillet and cooking the meat on the stove. (Broilers were not very efficient yet.) Pan-frying creates a deep, dark crust on the steak. The finishing touch is a thick pat of butter melted in the pan to collect the juices. So turn on the stove's vent (hint: you can expect some smoke), bake a potato, and get sizzling.

2 boneless top loin (shell or New York) or rib-eye steaks, about 14 ounces each
¾ teaspoon salt
½ teaspoon coarsely ground black pepper
4 tablespoons unsalted butter

1. Trim off some of the fat that surrounds the steaks and reserve. Season the steaks with the salt and pepper. Let stand at room temperature for 30 minutes.

2. Heat a large cast-iron skillet over medium-high heat. Use tongs to rub the fat inside a large cast-iron skillet to coat it—this should only take about 15 seconds. Discard the fat. Add the steaks and cook until the undersides are well-browned, about 4 minutes. Turn and cook until the other sides are well-browned and the steak feels only slightly resilient when pressed on top in the center, about 4 minutes more for medium-rare steak. (If you like your steak more well-done, reduce the heat to medium and continue cooking until the steak is done to your liking. When pressed, medium steak will feel moderately resilient, and well-done will feel firm.) Transfer each steak to a dinner plate.

3. Dip the bottom of the pan in a large bowl of cold water to cool the pan somewhat. (If you add the butter to the hot pan, it will burn.) Return to low heat. Add the butter and melt it, scraping up the browned bits in the pan with a wooden spoon. Pour and divide the butter equally over the steaks and serve hot.

NOTE: You will only be able to fit two steaks in the skillet. For hearty appetites, serve a steak to each person. Or, cut the steaks crosswise, across the grain, into ½-inch-thick slices, and stretch them to four servings.

YANKEE POT ROAST

This fork-tender pot roast has all of the old-fashioned flavors that make us hungry for simple American cooking. We did sneak a little wine in there—not very Yankee, but awfully good.

3 tablespoons bacon fat or vegetable oil
1 (3-pound) rump roast
Salt and freshly ground black pepper
3 medium carrots, 1 chopped, and 2 cut into 1-inch lengths
1 medium yellow onion, chopped
1 medium celery rib, chopped
1 garlic clove, minced
⅓ cup all-purpose flour
3 cups canned reduced-sodium beef broth
1 cup hearty red wine
1 tablespoon tomato paste
1 teaspoon dried thyme
1 bay leaf
3 medium red-skinned potatoes, scrubbed but not peeled, cut into halves lengthwise
2 medium turnips, peeled and cut into sixths

1. Position a rack in the center of the oven and preheat to 325°F.

2. Heat 2 tablespoons of bacon fat in a Dutch oven or flameproof casserole over medium-high heat. Season the rump roast with 1 teaspoon salt and ½ teaspoon pepper. Add to the Dutch oven and cook, turning occasionally, until browned on all sides, about 10 minutes. Transfer the rump roast to a plate.

3. Add the remaining 1 tablespoon fat to the Dutch oven. Add the chopped carrot, onion, and celery and cook, stirring occasionally, until softened, about 6 minutes. Stir in the garlic and cook until fragrant, about 1 minute. Sprinkle with the flour and stir well. Stir in the broth, wine, tomato paste, thyme, and bay leaf and bring to a simmer. Return the rump roast to the Dutch oven and cover.

4. Bake for 2 hours, turning the roast over after 1½ hours. Remove the Dutch oven from the oven. Add the cut carrots, potatoes, and turnips to the pot, submerging them in the cooking liquid. Return to the oven and cook until the meat and vegetables are tender, about 1 hour.

5. Transfer the rump roast to a deep serving platter and let stand 10 minutes. (Keep the vegetables warm in the gravy, covered.) Slice the rump roast. Use a slotted spoon to transfer the vegetables to the platter. Season the gravy with salt and pepper. Spoon some of the gravy over the roast and vegetables, and pour the remaining gravy into a sauceboat. Serve hot.

KITCHEN TIME MACHINE

To make a simple pot roast with onion gravy, use this time-tested favorite. Heat 1 tablespoon bacon fat or vegetable oil in a Dutch oven over medium-high heat. Brown a 3-pound rump roast in the fat, about 10 minutes. Add 1 (1-ounce) envelope dry onion soup mix combined with 2½ cups water. Bake, turning occasionally, until tender, about 3 hours. For gravy, remove the cooked roast to a platter. Mash 3 tablespoons unsalted butter and 3 tablespoons all-purpose flour together into a paste in a medium bowl. Whisk in about 1 cup of the cooking liquid, and whisk back into the Dutch oven. Simmer over medium-low heat for 10 minutes. You won't have enough liquid to cook the vegetables, so roast potatoes and carrots to serve on the side.

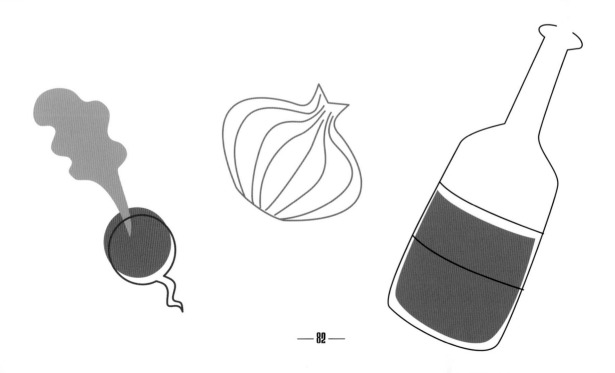

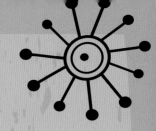

Dinner with the Family

Here is a delicious, middle-of-the-road meal that is guaranteed not to offend anyone, with a mellow soundtrack to match.

Iced tea

Beer

California Chablis or Burgundy

Iceberg Lettuce Wedge with Thousand Island Dressing (page 54)

Yankee Pot Roast (page 81)

Butter-Whipped Potatoes (page 135)

Mixed vegetables (carrots, peas, and corn) with butter

Tart-Tongued Lemon Meringue Pie (page 161)

Coffee and tea

CD PLAYLIST

Henry Mancini: *Midnight, Moonlight, and Magic*

Various: *Capitol Sings Rodgers and Hammerstein*

Ferrante and Teicher: *All-Time Greatest Hits*

THE ULTIMATE MEAT LOAF

How many millions of meat loaves were served every night by loving moms in the family dinner time zone that fell between homework and *Bonanza*? This is an over-the-top loaf that you will want to cook again and again . . . as long as you don't count the calories. If you ever doubted that fat makes food taste good, this recipe will have you kissing the sour cream container in thanks. So, when you just can't face ground turkey again, make this meat loaf, enriched with the ingredients of classic onion dip (including the potato chips!).

2 pounds ground round (85% lean)
1½ cups crushed potato chips
¾ cup sour cream
1 (1-ounce) envelope dry onion soup mix
2 large eggs, beaten

1. Position a rack in the center of the oven and preheat the oven to 350°F. Combine the ground round, potato chips, sour cream, onion soup mix, eggs, and ¼ cup water with your clean hands. Transfer to an 8½-by-4½-inch loaf pan.

2. Place on a baking sheet. Bake until an instant-read thermometer inserted in the center of the loaf reads 165°F, about 1¼ hours. Let stand 5 minutes. Drain off the excess fat, invert onto a serving platter, and slice.

Hamburglar

In 1961, there were only 100 McDonald's restaurants in the world. In 2010, there were more than 32,000.

SPAGHETTI AND MEATBALLS SOPHIA

MAKES 8 SERVINGS

This incredibly savory pasta dish stacks up: the sauce gets a porky measure of flavor from spareribs, and the meatballs sport three kinds of meat. This makes a lot, so you might want to plan on freezing some of the meatballs and sauce for another meal. We imagine that it's just the kind of Sunday dinner that Sophia Loren, the Italian dish of the Sixties and beyond, would make. After all, she herself said, "Everything you see I owe to spaghetti."

SAUCE

2 tablespoons olive oil
8 spareribs, cut into individual ribs (about 2¼ pounds)
1 teaspoon salt
½ teaspoon freshly ground black pepper
1 large yellow onion, chopped
1 large carrot, chopped
1 large celery rib with leaves, chopped
4 garlic cloves, finely chopped
2 (28-ounce) cans plum tomatoes in juice, preferably San Marzano, juices reserved, chopped
2 teaspoons dried basil
2 teaspoons dried oregano
½ teaspoon crushed hot red pepper flakes
2 bay leaves
1 cup hearty red wine

MEATBALLS

1½ cups fresh bread crumbs
½ cup whole milk
1 pound sweet Italian sausages, casings removed
1 pound ground round (85% lean)

1 pound ground veal
1 medium yellow onion, shredded on the large holes of a box grater
3 tablespoons finely chopped fresh parsley
2 large eggs, beaten
2 garlic cloves, minced
2 teaspoons salt
1 teaspoon freshly ground black pepper
2 tablespoons olive oil, as needed

2 pounds dried spaghetti
Freshly grated Parmesan cheese, for serving

1. To make the sauce, heat the oil in a very large (about 8 quarts) Dutch oven or flameproof casserole over medium-high heat. Season the spareribs with the salt and pepper. In batches, add the spareribs and cook, turning occasionally, until browned, about 6 minutes. Transfer to a plate.

2. Add the onion, carrot, and celery to the fat in the Dutch oven. Cover and cook, stirring occasionally, until softened, about 6 minutes. Stir in the garlic and cook, uncovered, until fragrant, about 1 minute. Stir in the tomatoes with their juices, the basil, oregano, hot pepper flakes, and bay leaves. Bring to a boil. Return the spareribs to the Dutch oven. Reduce the heat to medium-low and partially cover the pot. Cook, stirring occasionally, until the spareribs are barely tender, about 1¾ hours. If the sauce seems too thick, add water as needed.

3. To make the meatballs, combine the bread crumbs and milk in a large bowl. Let stand for 5 minutes to soften the crumbs. Add the sausages, ground round, ground veal, onion, parsley, eggs, garlic, salt, and pepper. Mix with your clean hands until combined. Shape into 24 meatballs and transfer to a large baking sheet.

4. Heat the oil in a large skillet over medium heat. In batches, add the meatballs and cook, turning occasionally, until lightly browned on all sides, about 6 minutes. The meatballs do not have to be cooked through, as they will cook more in the sauce. Transfer the browned meatballs to a platter. Pour the fat out of the skillet. Return the skillet to high heat and add the wine. Bring to a boil, stirring up the browned bits in the skillet with a wooden spoon. Stir into the spaghetti sauce.

5. When the spareribs are barely tender, add the meatballs to the sauce. Simmer until the spareribs are very tender and falling off the bone and the meatballs are cooked through, about 30 minutes more.

6. Meanwhile, bring a very large soup pot of salted water to a boil over high heat. Add the spaghetti and cook according to the package directions until al dente. Drain well and return to the pot.

7. Transfer the meatballs and spareribs to a large serving bowl. Toss the spaghetti in the pot with the sauce, and transfer to another large serving bowl. Serve hot, with the meatballs and spareribs, and Parmesan cheese passed on the side.

SOUPED-UP SWEDISH MEATBALLS

MAKES 4 TO 6 SERVINGS

Creamy and tender Swedish meatballs do double-duty in the busy cook's kitchen, as they are equally delectable speared with frill-picks and served with cocktails as they are spooned over egg noodles for supper. Here is the streamlined American rendition, which is about as Swedish as Sandy Koufax, but unless Ingmar Bergman is at the table, no one will complain.

1½ pounds ground round (85% lean) or 1 pound ground round and 1 pound ground pork
⅓ cup dried bread crumbs
1 large egg, beaten
¼ cup minced yellow onion
1½ teaspoons salt
½ teaspoon freshly ground black pepper
⅓ cup all-purpose flour
2 tablespoons vegetable oil
2 (10.7-ounce) cans condensed cream of mushroom soup
1 cup milk
Hot cooked egg noodles, for serving
Chopped fresh parsley, for garnish

1. Combine the ground round, bread crumbs, egg, onion, salt, and pepper in a large bowl. Mix with your hands until well combined. Using a heaping teaspoon for each, roll into 24 meatballs, and transfer to a baking sheet.

2. Spread the flour in a shallow dish. In batches, roll the meatballs in the flour, shaking off the excess flour and return them to the baking sheet.

3. Heat the oil in a large skillet over medium heat. In batches without crowding, add the meatballs and cook, turning occasionally, until browned, about 8 minutes. Using a slotted spoon, transfer to a plate.

4. Pour out any fat in the skillet. Add the soup and milk and bring to a simmer, stirring to combine and dislodge any browned bits in the skillet. Return the meatballs to the skillet and return to a simmer. Reduce the heat to low and simmer until the meatballs are cooked through, about 15 minutes. Serve hot, over the noodles, sprinkled with the parsley.

SPIKED SWEDISH MEATBALLS: Substitute 3 tablespoons dry sherry for an equal amount of the milk.

PUERTO RICAN PORK CHOPS WITH MOJO AND ONIONS

International food in the Sixties wasn't just inspired by Europe and Asia. Latin flavors were slowly salsa-ing their way into kitchens thanks in large part to the success of the 1961 movie *West Side Story* starring Natalie Wood as "Puerto Rican princess" Maria, and the popular new genre of music boogaloo, a fusion of mambo and soul. (In 1963, Ray Barretto's boogaloo hit "El Watusi" became the first Latin song to ever hit the *Billboard* charts.) These Puerto Rican-style pork chops, a.k.a. *chuletas*, are braised with sour orange and lots of onion. To really feel the heat, serve while belting out "I Feel Pretty."

2 tablespoons olive oil
1 teaspoon dried oregano
1 teaspoon ground cumin
Salt and freshly ground black pepper
4 center-cut loin pork chops on the bone, about 8 ounces each
2 medium yellow onions, cut into ¼-inch half-moons
1 garlic clove, finely chopped
⅔ cup fresh sour orange juice (available at Latino markets) or ½ cup fresh orange juice and 2 tablespoons fresh lime juice

1. Heat 1 tablespoon of oil in a large skillet over medium-high heat. Mix the oregano and cumin with ¾ teaspoon salt and ½ teaspoon pepper in a small bowl. Use the oregano mixture to season the pork chops. Add the pork chops to the skillet and cook, turning once, until the chops are browned, about 5 minutes, and the oregano and cumin. Transfer the pork chops to a plate.

2. Add the remaining 1 tablespoon oil to the skillet and heat. Add the onions and garlic and cook, stirring occasionally, until the onions soften, about 5 minutes. Return the pork chops to the skillet and cover them with the onions. Pour in the sour orange juice. Cover tightly and reduce the heat to medium-low. Simmer until the pork chops are tender and show no sign of pink when pierced at the bone, about 20 minutes. Transfer the pork chops to a platter. Cook the onion mixture in the skillet until the pan juices thicken, about 5 minutes. Season with salt and pepper. Pour the onion mixture over the pork chops and serve.

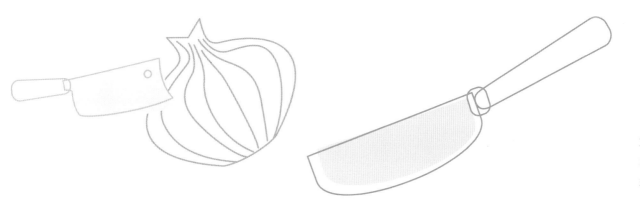

The Watusi

Dance crazes were all the rage in the Sixties. After the Twist, the king of solo dances was the Watusi. The Watusi was an international amalgamation: it was named for the African Batutsi tribe, accompanied by Latin-inspired boogaloo music, and most embraced by American surf culture. While Puerto Rican jazz musician Ray Barretto is most remembered for his version of "El Watusi," it was also recorded by Chubby Checker, Smokey Robinson and the Miracles, the Isley Brothers, the Vibrations, the Orlons, and Annette Funicello. In 1965, little Wednesday on *The Addams Family* danced the Watusi to a Lurch-produced single.

BANGERS AND MASH

MAKES 6 SERVINGS

There is no ignoring the British Invasion, the inundation of American music by the Beatles and other ground-breaking groups from the United Kingdom. If you are in a Carnaby Street mood, make these sausages in brown sauce, served over mashed potatoes, for the ultimate in English comfort food. This version uses beef to make the gravy, but hard apple cider, which is about as British a drink as they come, is also groovy.

1 tablespoon bacon fat or vegetable oil
12 British-style pork sausages (see Note) or sweet Italian sausages, pierced with a
    fork, about 1¼ pounds total
1 large onion, chopped
2 tablespoons all-purpose flour
2½ cups canned reduced-sodium beef broth
¾ cup dark or lager beer
Salt and freshly ground black pepper
Butter-Whipped Potatoes (page 135)
Whole-grain mustard, for serving

1. Position a rack in the center of the oven and preheat to 325°F.

2. Heat the fat in an ovenproof large skillet over medium-high heat. Add the sausages and cook, turning occasionally, until lightly browned, about 5 minutes. Transfer to a plate, leaving the fat in the pan.

3. Add the onion to the skillet and reduce the heat to medium. Cook, stirring often, until golden, about 5 minutes. Sprinkle in the flour and stir well. Stir in the broth and beer. Return the sausage to the skillet and bring the liquid to a simmer. Transfer to the oven and bake uncovered until the sausage is cooked through and the gravy has thickened, about 20 minutes. Season with salt and pepper.

4. Spoon the potatoes onto dinner plates, and top with the sausages and gravy. Serve hot with the mustard.

NOTE: British cooks would use Cumberland sausages, a mild, sage-flavored sausage. Any kind of lightly seasoned sausage in large links will do.

BAKED HAM WITH SODA POP GLAZE

In the Sixties, Spam wasn't the only "miracle meat in a can" (although they had sold *one billion* cans by 1959). Larger canned hams were quite popular, and proffered a distinct taste thanks to their syrupy preservatives. It's a sweet glaze we miss, but not even in the name of authenticity can we recommend canned ham over natural. Therefore, this recipe has the same flavors that you would be likely to find on the canned ham, only applied to a bone-in half ham. Welcome back, pineapple and maraschino cherries—we've missed you!

1 (8-pound) smoked ham on the bone, preferably shank end
About 40 whole cloves
1 (12-ounce) can ginger ale or lemon-lime soda
1 (20-ounce) can pineapple slices
10 maraschino cherries

1. Position a rack in the center of the oven and preheat the oven to 325ºF. Line a large roasting pan with aluminum foil.

2. If the ham has the thick rind attached, trim most of it off, leaving a thin layer of fat. Score the ham in a diamond pattern. Insert the cloves evenly over the ham. Stand the ham in the pan, cut side down. Pour the ginger ale all over the ham. Tent the ham with foil.

3. Bake, basting with the soda in the pan about every 45 minutes, for 3 hours. If the pan juices evaporate into a glaze and threaten to burn, moisten them with 1 cup of water. Remove the pan with the ham from the oven. Using wooden toothpicks, secure the pineapple slices and cherries to the ham. Baste with the pan juices, and return to the oven. Continue baking until an instant-read thermometer inserted in the thickest part of the ham, without touching a bone, reads 140ºF, about 1 hour more.

4. Let the ham stand at room temperature for 15 minutes. Carve the ham and serve warm.

LEG OF LAMB WITH GRAVY AND MINT JELLY

For most Americans living in the Sixties, lamb existed merely as an excuse to serve mint jelly. Midcentury cooks would have made it like this—without the Mediterranean influences that have made lamb more popular in subsequent years. So, here is lamb that might have come from Mom's recipe box, without a drop of wine, but still with plenty of flavor.

1 (5½- to 6-pound) leg of lamb, trimmed of excess fat
1 large garlic clove, cut into 12 slivers
1 lemon, cut in half
1 tablespoon vegetable oil
1 teaspoon dried rosemary
1 teaspoon dried thyme
Salt and freshly ground black pepper
1 small yellow onion, coarsely chopped
1 small carrot, coarsely chopped
1 small celery rib, coarsely chopped
2 tablespoons unsalted butter
2 tablespoons all-purpose flour
Mint jelly, for serving

1. Using the tip of a sharp knife, poke 12 incisions all over the lamb, spacing them evenly apart. Insert a garlic sliver into each incision. Rub the lemon halves over the lamb, squeezing out the juice. Rub the lamb with the oil. Combine the rosemary, thyme, 1 teaspoon salt, and ½ teaspoon pepper and rub evenly over the lamb. Let stand, uncovered, at room temperature for 1 hour.

2. Position a rack in the center of the oven and preheat the oven to 450°F. Lightly oil a roasting pan large enough to hold the lamb.

3. Place the lamb in the roasting pan. Scatter the onion, carrot, and celery around the lamb. Roast for 15 minutes. Reduce the oven temperature to 350°F. Roast for 45 minutes. Add ½ cup water to the pan. Continue roasting until an instant-read thermometer inserted into the center of the thickest part of the lamb reads 130°F, about 30 minutes more for medium-rare lamb. Transfer the lamb to a platter. Set aside while making the gravy. The lamb should stand for at least 15 minutes before carving.

4. Pour the vegetables from the pan into a wire sieve set over a large glass measuring cup. Strain, pressing hard on the vegetables. Let stand a few minutes, and skim off and discard the fat from the surface of the pan juices. Add enough water to the juices to make 1½ cups.

5. Place the roasting pan over medium heat on the stove. Add and melt the butter in the pan. Sprinkle in the flour and whisk until smooth, scraping up any browned bits in the pan. Whisk in the pan juices and bring to a boil. Reduce the heat to medium-low and cook until lightly thickened and no flour taste remains, about 5 minutes. Season with salt and pepper. Pour into a sauceboat.

6. Carve the lamb parallel to the bone. Serve hot, with the gravy and mint jelly.

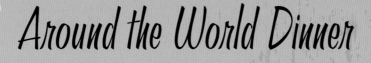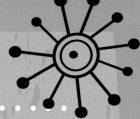

Around the World Dinner

Here is a recreation of the infamous dinner on the TV series *Mad Men*, an exemplary case of Sixties culture in today's lifestyle.

Daiquiris (page 188)

Rumaki-a-rama (page 39)*

Blender Gazpacho (page 58)

Leg of Lamb with Gravy and Mint Jelly (page 94)
Grandmother's Noodles with Sour Cream and Poppy Seeds (page 133)
Green beans sautéed with butter and almonds
Buttermilk Dinner Rolls (page 142)

Heineken beer
French Burgundy (California pinot noir is a good substitute.)

Cherries Jubiliee (page 173)
Coffee and tea
Assorted liqueurs
***Betty mentions this as part of her seated dinner, but it is strictly finger food.**

CD PLAYLIST

Ultra-Lounge, *Bachelor Pad Royale*
Cocktail Mix, *Martini Madness*
Esquivel, *Infinity in Sound, Vol. 1-2*

MISS ROASTER CHICKEN

MAKES 2 TO 4 SERVINGS

One of the most famous (and highly enjoyable) episodes of Julia Child's groundbreaking television show *The French Chef* is "To Roast a Chicken" from Season 1 in 1963. In it, Julia opens the show behind a line of headless poultry, introducing viewers to "the Chicken Sisters" before shimmying to her own theme music. She laments, "We're always boiling and broiling and grilling and baking and braising and barbecuing chicken, but what's ever happened to the roast chicken?" Julia elevated many a Sunday dinner when she taught her viewers how to prepare "Miss Roaster." The hilarious clip (Julia pretends the uncooked bird has won a beauty pageant and sings out its measurements: "14-15-14!") is well worth looking up online. The chicken—plump and juicy with a nice, golden brown burnished skin—is even worthier.

1 whole chicken (about 4 pounds), giblets discarded
2 tablespoons unsalted butter, at room temperature
Salt and freshly ground black pepper
1 small onion, cut in half
3 medium red-skinned potatoes, cut lengthwise into halves
3 medium carrots, cut into 2-inch lengths

1. Position a rack in the center of the oven and preheat the oven to 425°F.

2. Rub the outside of the chicken with the butter. Season the chicken, inside and out, with 1 teaspoon salt and ½ teaspoon pepper. Stuff the onion in the body cavity.

3. Place the chicken, breast down, in a roasting rack in a roasting pan. Roast for 20 minutes. Remove the pan with the chicken from the stove. Turn the chicken on its back. Baste with the pan juices. Add the potatoes and carrots around the chicken on the rack, and stir to coat with the pan juices. Return to the oven and continue baking, stirring the vegetables after 30 minutes, until the vegetables are tender and an instant-read thermometer inserted in the thickest part of the breast without touching a bone reads 165°F, 50 minutes to 1 hour. Transfer the vegetables to a serving bowl, season with salt and pepper, and cover with aluminum foil to keep warm. Transfer the chicken to a serving platter and let stand, uncovered, for 10 minutes.

4. Carve the chicken and let the chicken meat fall into the collected juices in the platter. Serve the chicken hot, with the vegetables.

POTATO CHIP BAKED CHICKEN

Many recipe books from the Sixties were really clever sales pitches published by food manufacturers hoping to convince cooks to use their products in new, exciting, and profit-rising ways. The "Heinz Home Economics Department" suggested spicing up frozen spinach with $2/3$ cup of their tomato ketchup. Basting a duck in 7Up would "take away any 'gamey' taste" (so promised the soda maker). One nontraditional suggestion we heartily endorse is the marriage of potato chips and chicken. The salty crushed chips are a wonderful coating for baked poultry. You can also use barbecue-flavored chips, but then don't season the batter.

8 tablespoons (1 stick) unsalted butter, melted
2 garlic cloves, crushed through a press
1 teaspoon dried thyme
1 teaspoon dried rosemary
½ teaspoon freshly ground black pepper
2 cups (6 ounces) finely crushed potato chips (see Note)
1 whole chicken (about 4 pounds), cut into 8 serving pieces, skin removed and giblets discarded

1. Position a rack in the center of the oven and preheat to 350°F. Lightly oil a 15-by-10-inch baking dish.

2. Combine the butter, garlic, thyme, rosemary, and pepper in a shallow dish. Spread the potato chips in another dish. Roll each piece of chicken in the butter mixture and then coat with the potato chips, patting the chips on to help them adhere. Place in the baking dish. Drizzle any of the remaining butter mixture on top of the chicken.

3. Bake until an instant-read thermometer inserted in the thickest part of a chicken breast half reads 170°F, about 50 minutes. Serve hot or at room temperature.

NOTE: To crush the potato chips, transfer them to a large plastic bag and whack with a rolling pin.

SOULFUL FRIED CHICKEN

In the past, fried chicken required very few ingredients, and we think it is the better for it. Except for the residents of New Orleans, midcentury Southerners viewed most spices with suspicion; they would not recognize today's fired-up birds. One very important thing to remember is the size of the chicken. Only recently has the average chicken been bred to proportions resembling a Coupe de Ville. These huge birds are not suited for frying, as the crust burns by the time the pieces cook through. You can find properly sized small birds at natural food stores and some supermarkets.

1 quart buttermilk
¼ cup plus ¾ teaspoons salt, divided
1 (3½-pound) chicken, giblets discarded, cut into 2 each wings, drumsticks, thighs, and breast halves, with each breast half cut crosswise to make a total of 10 chicken pieces
1½ cups all-purpose flour
1 teaspoon baking powder
1 teaspoon freshly ground black pepper
Vegetable oil, for deep-frying (see Note)

1. Whisk the buttermilk and ¼ cup of salt together in a large, deep nonreactive bowl to dissolve the salt. Add the chicken and submerge in the buttermilk mixture. Cover with plastic wrap and refrigerate for at least 3 and up to 4 hours.

2. Mix the flour, baking powder, the remaining ¾ teaspoon salt, and the pepper together in a large bowl. One piece at a time, remove the chicken from the buttermilk mixture, shaking off the excess liquid, and roll in the flour mixture. Transfer to a baking sheet. Let the coated chicken stand at room temperature to set the coating, about 15 minutes.

3. Pour oil into a heavy-bottomed large skillet (preferably cast iron) to come about halfway up the sides. Heat over high heat until the oil is shimmering or reads 350°F on a deep-frying thermometer. Add the breast pieces to the skillet and cook over high heat until the undersides are golden, about 3 minutes. Cover the skillet and cook for 5 minutes. Turn the chicken and cook, uncovered, turning occasionally, until the chicken is crisp and golden brown, and an instant-read thermometer inserted in the thickest part of a piece reads 165°F, about 7 minutes longer. (Remove the chicken from the oil to test.) During frying, adjust the heat as needed so bubbles are active around the perimeter of the chicken, but the chicken isn't cooking too rapidly. Transfer to a wire cake rack set over a rimmed baking sheet to drain. Repeat with the dark meat chicken pieces. Serve warm.

NOTE: If you wish, substitute up to one-half of the vegetable oil with an equal amount of lard or bacon fat.

Soul Food

In a nod to soul music—the combination of gospel and R&B—"soul food" was christened in the Sixties to denote the culinary traditions of African American culture. While every region has its own soulful specialties, soul food is at its essence warm, comforting family food.

CHICKEN DIVAN

Casseroles, those one-dish wonders of the kitchen, reached their peak in the early Sixties. With more and more women entering the work force, how to cook a fast meal was a hot topic. Very often, a can of soup substituted for homemade sauce, a practice that is fine on occasion (like for Souped-Up Swedish Meatballs, page 89), but shouldn't become a way of life. One of the most frequent victims of favorites made easier (but certainly not better) was chicken Divan, a lovely dish of sauced chicken over broccoli that made the New York restaurant Divan Parisienne justly famous. Here's the original from-scratch recipe.

3 chicken breast halves with skin and bones (about 13 ounces each)
1¾ cups canned reduced-sodium chicken broth
½ small yellow onion
1 pinch of dried thyme
12 ounces broccoli crowns, cut into florets (about 4 cups)
6 tablespoons (¾ stick) unsalted butter, divided, plus more for the baking dish
⅓ cup all-purpose flour
½ cup heavy cream
4 large egg yolks
2 tablespoons dry sherry
1 tablespoon fresh lemon juice
½ teaspoon Worcestershire sauce
Salt and freshly ground black pepper
½ cup (2 ounces) freshly grated Parmesan cheese

1. Place the chicken, broth, and onion in a large saucepan and add enough cold water to cover the chicken by 1 inch. Bring to a simmer over high heat, skimming off any foam that rises to the surface. Add the thyme. Reduce the heat to medium-low. Simmer until the chicken shows no sign of pink when pierced at the thickest part near a bone, about 40 minutes.

2. Transfer the chicken to a carving board and let cool until easy to handle. Remove the skin and bones, and pull the chicken meat into bite-sized pieces. Pour the broth into a bowl and let stand 5 minutes. Skim off the fat from the surface. Measure 2½ cups chicken broth; reserve the remaining broth for another use.

3. Lightly butter a 13-by-9-inch flameproof baking dish. Bring a large pot of salted water to a boil over high heat. Add the broccoli and cook until crisp-tender, about 5 minutes. Drain and rinse under cold running water. Drain again. Pat completely dry with clean kitchen towels. Spread the broccoli in the baking dish. Top with the chicken.

4. Melt 5 tablespoons of butter in a medium saucepan over medium-low heat. Whisk in the flour. Let bubble without browning for 1 minute. Whisk in the measured broth and cream. Bring to a simmer over medium heat, whisking often. Return the heat to medium-low and simmer, whisking often, until lightly thickened, about 3 minutes.

5. Whisk the yolks in a medium bowl. Gradually whisk in the hot sauce. Return to the saucepan and add the sherry, lemon juice, and Worcestershire sauce. Whisk over medium-low heat until thickened, without letting the sauce come to a simmer, about 2 minutes. Season with salt and pepper. Pour over the chicken and broccoli. (The chicken Divan can be prepared, ahead, cooled, covered, and refrigerated, up to 4 hours ahead.)

6. Position a rack in the center of the oven and preheat to 400°F. Sprinkle the Parmesan on top, then dot with the remaining 1 tablespoon butter. Bake until the sauce is bubbling and the top is golden, about 20 minutes (or 25 minutes if previously refrigerated). Let stand a few minutes, then serve hot.

KITCHEN TIME MACHINE

Spread 1 (10-ounce) package thawed frozen broccoli spears in a 9-inch pie plate. Top with 2 cups chopped cooked chicken. Mix 1 (10.75-ounce) can cream of chicken soup with ⅓ cup shredded sharp Cheddar cheese, and pour over the chicken. Mix 2 tablespoons dried bread crumbs and 1 tablespoon melted butter and sprinkle on top. Bake in a preheated 425°F oven until bubbling, about 20 minutes.

CHICKEN BREASTS KIEV

Even the most *chi-chi* Sixties restaurants passed out bibs with their chicken Kiev—a dish of deep-fried chicken breasts filled with herb butter that tended to squirt like a geyser if you knifed it just so. There are recipes for baked Kiev, but a leisurely bath in hot oil is the only way to give the chicken its gorgeous crunchy coating. We recommend baked chicken Kiev with the same enthusiasm that we recommend Tang over fresh orange juice.

6 tablespoons unsalted butter, at room temperature
2 teaspoons minced fresh chives
2 teaspoons minced fresh tarragon
Grated zest of 1 lemon
1 garlic clove, crushed through a press
Salt and freshly ground black pepper
6 boneless and skinless chicken breast halves (about 8 ounces each)
3 large eggs
½ cup all-purpose flour
¾ cup dried bread crumbs
Vegetable oil, for deep-frying
Lemon wedges, for serving

1. Mix the butter, chives, tarragon, lemon zest, and garlic together in a small bowl. Season with salt and pepper. Cover and refrigerate just until firm enough to shape, about 30 minutes. Shape the butter mixture into 6 finger-sized portions. Place on a waxed paper–lined plate and refrigerate until firm, about 30 minutes more.

2. One at a time, place a chicken breast half between two sheets of plastic wrap. Pound with the flat side of a meat pounder (or a rolling pin) until the flesh is pounded into a fan shape about 5 inches wide, 6 inches long, and ½ inch thick. Place a butter "finger" in the bottom third of the pounded chicken. Fold in the sides, then roll up from the bottom to from a packet and entirely enclose the butter. The flesh should stick to itself, but if necessary, close up the packet with a wooden toothpick.

3. Line a baking sheet with waxed paper. Beat the eggs in a shallow bowl with a pinch of salt. Mix the flour in another shallow bowl with ½ teaspoon salt and ¼ teaspoon pepper. Spread the bread crumbs in a third shallow bowl. One at a time, roll a chicken packet in the egg mixture, then the flour mixture, then the bread crumbs to coat. Place on the baking sheet. Refrigerate for 30 minutes to get the coating.

4. Choose a large, wide saucepan big enough to hold the breasts without crowding. Pour enough oil to come 3 inches up the side of the pan and heat over high heat to 350ºF on a deep-frying thermometer. Carefully add the chicken to the hot oil and cook adjusting the heat as needed to keep the breasts steadily cooking but not too quickly, until the crust is deep golden brown, about 7 minutes. Use a slotted spoon to transfer the chicken to a wire cake rack set over a rimmed baking sheet to drain briefly.

5. Transfer each piece to a dinner plate, add the lemon wedges, and serve hot.

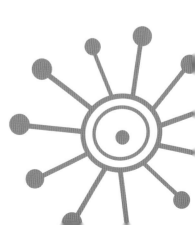

CHICKEN À LA KING

This is another old favorite (dating back to the late 1800s) that was newly discovered by housewives who reinvented it with canned soup. The from-scratch version is very good, and deserves to be rediscovered again. In spite of its royal name, it is an easy weeknight dish, and while you could prepare chicken breast and broth as described in the Chicken Divan on page 102, here is a version that uses today's store-bought rotisserie chicken. Or use leftover chicken or turkey, if you have some. And while many folks serve it over noodles or rice, we love it with biscuits.

¼ cup unsalted butter, divided
½ cup (½-inch) diced red bell pepper
10 ounces white mushrooms, sliced
¼ cup chopped shallots
¼ cup all-purpose flour
1⅔ cups canned reduced-sodium chicken broth
1 cup half-and-half
⅓ cup dry sherry
Salt and freshly ground black pepper
3 cups (15 ounces) bite-sized cooked chicken (from 1 large rotisserie chicken)
½ cup thawed frozen baby peas (optional)
6 Homemade Biscuits (page 139), split

1. Melt 2 tablespoons of the butter in a large skillet over medium heat. Add the red pepper and cook, stirring occasionally, until softened, about 2 minutes. Add the mushrooms and cook, stirring occasionally, until they are sizzling in their own juices, about 5 minutes. Stir in the shallots and cook until they soften, about 1 minute.

2. Stir in the remaining 2 tablespoons of butter and let it melt. Sprinkle in the flour and stir well. Add the broth,

half-and-half, and sherry and stir well. Bring to a simmer and reduce the heat to medium-low. Simmer, stirring often, until the sauce is lightly thickened and no raw flour taste remains, about 5 minutes. Season with salt and pepper.

3. Stir in the chicken and peas, if using, and cook just until heated through, about 3 minutes. To serve, place a biscuit half on each of 6 dinner plates. Divide the chicken mixture equally over the biscuit halves, and add a biscuit top to each. Serve hot.

KITCHEN TIME MACHINE

To make the classic can-of-soup version, whisk 1 (10.75-ounce) can cream of mushroom soup, 1 (10.75-ounce) can cream of chicken soup, and 2 cups whole milk in a large skillet over medium heat until simmering. Add 3 cups bite-sized pieces cooked chicken, 1 (4-ounce) jar drained chopped pimentos, and 1 cup thawed frozen baby peas. Cook, stirring occasionally, until heated through, about 5 minutes. Serve hot, over cooked egg noodles.

ROAST TURKEY WITH GRAVY

MAKES ABOUT 18 SERVINGS WITH ABOUT 7 CUPS GRAVY

Ah, Thanksgiving dinner, the scene for family bonding and unbonding. With high hopes that your holiday meal will be free of arguments over the qualities of sweet potatoes, here is the best way to roast turkey and make gravy that we know. While most Sixties families used a frozen turkey, ignore this tradition and go for a fresh bird. And be very wary of using a disposable aluminum foil pan. Unless you use a sturdy roasting pan, half of your delicious gravy could end up on the floor.

1 fresh turkey (about 18 pounds)
Everyone Loves It Stuffing (page 138), freshly made and warm
8 tablespoons (1 stick) unsalted butter, at room temperature, plus more if needed
Salt and freshly ground black pepper
1 tablespoon vegetable oil
1 medium onion, chopped
1 medium celery rib with leaves, chopped
1 quart chicken broth
¼ teaspoon dried thyme
1 small bay leaf
¾ cup all-purpose flour

1. Position a rack in the lowest position of the oven and preheat to 325°F. Reserve the turkey neck and giblets to use in gravy or stock. Pull out the pads of yellow fat at either side of the tail and reserve. Rinse the turkey inside and out with cold water. Pat the turkey skin dry. Turn the turkey on its breast. Loosely fill the neck cavity with stuffing. Using a thin wooden or metal skewer, pin the turkey's neck skin to the back. Fold the turkey's wings akimbo behind the back or tie to the body with kitchen string. Loosely fill the large body cavity with stuffing. Place any remaining stuffing in a lightly buttered baking dish, cover with aluminum foil, and refrigerate to bake later as a side dish. Place the drumsticks in the hock lock or tie together with kitchen

string. Rub all over with the softened butter. Season the outside of the bird with 1½ teaspoons salt and ½ teaspoon pepper.

2. Place the turkey, breast side up, on a rack in a large roasting pan. Tightly cover the breast area with aluminum foil. Add 2 cups of water and the reserved turkey fat to the pan.

3. Roast the turkey, basting whenever you feel like (but no more than every 45 minutes), until a meat thermometer inserted in the meaty part of the thigh (but not touching a bone) reads 180°F degrees and the stuffing is at least 160°F, about 4¼ hours. (See Estimated Turkey Roasting Times on page 110.) Whenever the pan drippings evaporate, add water to moisten them (about 1½ cups at a time). *Remove the foil* during the last hour to allow the skin to brown, and be sure to baste at least once after the foil is removed.

4. Meanwhile, to make turkey stock, use a heavy knife to chop the neck into 2- to 3-inch chunks. Heat the vegetable oil in a large saucepan over medium-high heat. Add the chopped neck, gizzard, and heart and cook, turning occasionally, until browned, about 8 minutes. Add the onion and celery and cook, stirring occasionally, until softened, about 5 minutes. Add the broth and enough water to cover the turkey parts by 1 inch. Bring to a boil over high heat, skimming off any foam that rises to the surface. Add the thyme and bay leaf. Simmer while the turkey is roasting, at least 2 and up to 4 hours. Strain into a large bowl. Let stand 5 minutes, then skim off the fat and reserve from the surface. Pour the skimmed fat into the turkey roasting pan. (Yes, you have to make the turkey stock. It is the secret to great gravy.)

5. Transfer the turkey to a large serving platter and let it stand for at least 20 minutes before carving. (Use the empty oven to bake the side dishes. Pour ½ cup turkey broth over the stuffing in the baking dish, Cover with aluminum foil, and bake until heated through, about 30 minutes.)

6. Meanwhile, pour the drippings from the roasting pan into a gravy separator. Let stand 5 minutes; then pour off the pan drippings into a 2-quart glass measuring cup, leaving the fat in the separator. Measure ¾ cup fat, adding melted butter, if needed. Add enough turkey stock to the skimmed drippings to make 8 cups total.

7. Place the roasting pan over two stove burners on medium heat and add the ¾ cup of turkey fat. Add the flour and whisk, scraping up the browned bits on the bottom of the pan with a flat roux whisk. Cook until the flour is lightly browned, about 2 minutes. Whisk in the turkey stock mixture. Bring to a boil. Reduce the heat to low and cook, whisking often, until the gravy thickens and no trace of raw flour flavor remains, about 10 minutes. Season with salt and pepper. Transfer the gravy to a large gravy boat. Carve the turkey and serve the gravy alongside.

Estimated Turkey Roasting Times

(Oven Temperature 325°F)
An 18-pound turkey is large enough to make an impressive appearance at the table, and is sure to provide plenty of leftovers for up to 12 people. If you want to use a turkey with a different weight, use this chart. Add an extra 30 minutes to the roasting time to allow for variations in roasting conditions. It's better to have a bird done ahead of time than to keep everyone waiting and hungry for the bird to finish roasting.

Unstuffed Turkey

8 to 12 pounds	$2^3/_4$ to 3 hours
12 to 14 pounds	3 to $3^3/_4$ hours
14 to 18 pounds	$3^3/_4$ to $4^1/_4$ hours
18 to 20 pounds	$4^1/_4$ to $4^1/_2$ hours
20 to 24 pounds	$4^1/_2$ to 5 hours

Stuffed Turkey

8 to 12 pounds	3 to $3^1/_2$ hours
12 to 14 pounds	$3^1/_2$ to 4 hours
14 to 18 pounds	4 to $4^1/_4$ hours
18 to 20 pounds	$4^1/_4$ to $4^3/_4$ hours
20 to 24 pounds	$4^3/_4$ to $5^1/_4$ hours

NOT-QUITE FISH STICKS

MAKES 4 SERVINGS

Although frozen fish sticks were first introduced in the early 1950s, there weren't enough freezers in grocery stores or homes to make much room for them. By the 1960s, however, houses got bigger kitchens, home freezer sales quadrupled, and frozen fish stick sales tripled (we suppose they didn't quadruple because people still had to make room for ice cream!). Many of us were served the breaded fish "fingers" twice on Fridays—once at school and again for dinner. Here's our homemade, not-frozen version, crunchy coating still included.

1½ pounds sole fillets
Salt and freshly ground black pepper
½ cup all-purpose flour
2 large eggs
1 cup dried bread crumbs
Vegetable oil, for deep-frying
Tartar sauce, for serving
Lemon wedges, for serving

1. Cut the sole crosswise on a diagonal into ½-inch-wide strips. Season with ½ teaspoon salt and ¼ teaspoon pepper.

2. Spread the flour in a shallow dish. Beat the eggs in a second shallow dish. Spread the bread crumbs in a third dish. In batches, dip the fish strips in the flour, and shake off the excess flour. Dip in the eggs to coat, letting the excess egg drip off. Then roll in the bread crumbs to coat. Transfer to a rimmed baking sheet. Let stand while heating the oil.

3. Preheat the oven to 200°F. Line a rimmed baking sheet with a brown paper bag. Pour enough oil to come about ½ inch up the sides of a large skillet and heat over high heat until the oil is shimmering.

4. In batches without crowding, add the fish strips to the oil and cook until golden brown, about 1½ minutes. Using a wire spider or slotted spoon, transfer to the paper-lined baking sheet and keep warm in the oven while frying the remaining fish.

5. Serve hot, with the tartar sauce and lemon wedges.

DUCK À L'ORANGE

· · · · · · · · · · ·
MAKES 2 TO 4 SERVINGS
· · · · · · · · · · ·

Continental cuisine was a savory mélange of dishes, living together in harmony on a menu even if they didn't always peacefully coexist on the European continent (see World War I and World War II). The Kiev would lay down with the scampi, with red-jacketed, accented waiters acting as ambassadors to this comfortable world of wine, chafing dishes, and candlelight. Duck à l'orange, roast duck in orange sauce, often represented the French faction on Continental menus. And now you can make it *chez nous.*

1 whole duck (5 to 6 pounds), giblets reserved (discard the liver or reserve for another use)
Salt and freshly ground black pepper
1¾ cups canned reduced-sodium chicken broth
2 small onions, each cut into quarters, divided
⅛ teaspoon dried thyme
1 bay leaf
3 navel oranges
3 tablespoons sugar
2 tablespoons orange liqueur, such as Grand Marnier
2 tablespoons fresh lemon juice

1. The day before serving, pull out and reserve the fat inside the body cavity at the tail end of the duck. Using a heavy knife or kitchen shears, chop off the wing tips at the first joint. Chop the wing tips and neck into 2-inch chunks. Cover and refrigerate with heart and gizzard. (Discard the liver or reserve for another use.)

2. Sprinkle the duck inside and out with 1½ teaspoons salt and ½ teaspoon pepper. Place the duck on a wire rack on a rimmed baking sheet. Refrigerate for 24 hours. (This dries the skin and helps the duck release its fat.)

3. Heat the duck fat in a medium saucepan over medium-high heat until it begins to melt, about 3 minutes. Add the wing tips, neck, heart, and gizzard and cook until browned, about 5 minutes. Add the broth, 1 cup water, and 1 quartered onion. Bring to a simmer, skimming off any foam that rises to the surface. Add the thyme and bay leaf. Simmer until reduced to about 2 cups, about 1 hour. Strain into a bowl. Let stand a few minutes, then skim off any fat from the surface. (The duck stock can be cooled, covered, and refrigerated, for up to 1 day.)

4. Position a rack in the center of the oven and preheat to 400°F. Using the tines of a meat fork, pierce the duck skin all over, taking care not to go into the flesh. Be sure to pierce the fattiest areas near the thighs and wings. Stuff the body cavity of the duck with the remaining onion and ½ orange, cut into a few wedges. Place the duck on a roasting rack in a roasting pan, breast side down. Roast for 45 minutes. Every 15 minutes or so during roasting, use a bulb baster to remove accumulated fat from the pan (there will be quite a lot), and pierce the skin with the tines of the meat fork. Turn the duck breast side up and continue roasting (and removing the fat and piercing the skin) until an instant-read thermometer inserted in the thickest part of the breast reads 170°F, about 45 minutes longer.

5. Meanwhile, remove the orange zest from 1 of the remaining oranges with a vegetable peeler, and cut into ⅛-inch-wide strips. Scrape off any bits of yellow pith with the edge of a paring knife, if needed. Place in a small saucepan and cover with cold water. Bring to a boil and cook for 3 minutes. Drain, rinse under cold water, and pat dry with paper towels.

6. Stir the sugar and ¼ cup water in a heavy-bottomed small saucepan over high heat until the sugar dissolves. Cook without stirring, occasionally swirling the pan by its handle, until the sugar is smoking and caramelized to the color of a copper penny, about 3 minutes. Pour in the liqueur, then the duck stock, orange juice, and lemon juice. Bring to a boil, stirring until the caramel is dissolved. Remove from the heat.

7. When the duck is done, drain the juices from the body cavity into a bowl, then add the juices to the stock mixture. Transfer the duck to a carving board. Pour out the fat in the pan (see Note), leaving any browned bits in the pan. Place the pan over high heat on the stove. Pour in the stock mixture. Bring to a boil and cook, scraping up any browned bits in the pan with a wooden spatula, until the liquid reduces to about ¾ cup, about 5 minutes. Season with salt and pepper.

8. Cut the duck into quarters. Serve hot, with the sauce spooned on top and garnished with the orange zest strips.

NOTE: The rendered duck fat from the roasting pan can be stored in a covered container in the refrigerator for up to 1 month or frozen for up to 3 months. Like bacon fat, gourmet cooks know that it is a great medium for sautéing meat, poultry, and vegetables, especially potatoes.

Continental Cuisine for Sophisticates

Put a candle in a wine bottle, lower the lights, and take a trip to Europe without leaving the comfort of your home.

Negronis (page 197)

Shrimp Cocktail with Bloody Mary Sauce (page 42)

Duck à l'Orange (page 112)
Wild rice with toasted pine nuts
Steamed carrots

Crêpes Bardot (page 174)
Coffee
Grand Marnier

CD PLAYLIST

Ultra-Lounge, Vol. 10, *Bachelor in Paris*
Juliette Gréco, *Les Plus Grandes Chansons*
Putumayo Presents: *French Café*

SHRIMP SCAMPI

MAKES 4 SERVINGS

Whether you're preparing an impressive feast for your business associates or just want to prepare a quick dinner at home, shrimp scampi rarely disappoints. Ignore the fact that "scampi" means langoustine (also called the Dublin Bay prawn)—a kind of small, clawless lobster that isn't easily found on these shores—and does not refer to a specific recipe. Every chef prepares scampi differently, and this version combines elements from our favorites for plump shrimp in a garlicky butter sauce that begs to be soaked with bread. Steamed rice and asparagus would be nice side dishes.

2 tablespoons olive oil
1½ pounds extra large (21 to 25 count) shrimp, peeled and deveined
Salt and freshly ground black pepper
4 tablespoons (½ stick) unsalted butter, divided
1 garlic clove, finely chopped
¾ cup dry white wine, such as pinot grigio
Grated zest of ½ lemon
2 tablespoons fresh lemon juice
1½ teaspoons all-purpose flour
Finely chopped fresh parsley, for garnish

1. Heat the oil in a large skillet over medium-high heat. Season the shrimp with ¼ teaspoon salt and ¼ teaspoon pepper. Add the shrimp and cook, stirring occasionally, until they are firm and opaque, about 3 minutes. Use a slotted spoon to transfer the shrimp to a platter.

2. Add 2 tablespoons of butter and the garlic together to the skillet and return to medium heat. Cook, stirring often, until the garlic is softened but not browned, about 1 minute. Combine the wine, lemon zest and juice in a small bowl, sprinkle in the flour, and whisk to dissolve the flour. Pour into the skillet and bring to a boil, scraping up any browned bits in the skillet with a wooden spoon. Cook until slightly thickened, about 1 minute. Return the shrimp to the skillet and cook for 1 minute. Remove from the heat and stir in the remaining 2 tablespoons butter. Season with salt and pepper.

3. Divide the scampi equally among four dinner plates, sprinkle with the parsley, and serve.

CRAB-STUFFED SHRIMP

MAKES 4 SERVINGS

While stuffing a roast bird has been around since the dawn of time, stuffing like (and not so alike) foods into one another was a Sixties specialty. Gelatin was stuffed with vegetables, eggs were stuffed with mushrooms, and perhaps most successfully shrimp was stuffed with crab. It is one of Rick's favorite childhood dishes, remembered from eating out at white-tablecloth restaurants on San Francisco's Fisherman's Wharf.

3 tablespoons unsalted butter, divided
3 tablespoons minced scallion, white and pale green parts only
1 garlic clove, minced
8 ounces crabmeat, picked over for cartilage and shells
1 cup fresh bread crumbs, divided
¼ cup mayonnaise
2 tablespoons chopped fresh parsley, plus more for garnish
1 teaspoon dried oregano
½ teaspoon hot red pepper sauce
Salt
16 jumbo shrimp, peeled, butterflied and deveined, with the tail segments attached
1 tablespoon olive oil
½ cup dry white wine, such as pinot grigio
Lemon wedges, for serving

1. Melt 1 tablespoon of butter in a medium skillet over medium heat. Add the scallion and garlic and cook, stirring often, until wilted, about 2 minutes. Scrape into a medium bowl and let cool slightly.

2. Add the crabmeat, ¾ cup of bread crumbs, mayonnaise, parsley, oregano, hot red pepper sauce, and mix. Season the crab mixture with salt. Divide into 16 portions.

3. Open the butterflied shrimp, cut side up. Top each shrimp with a portion of the crab mixture, shaping the filling to the shrimp. Place the shrimp side by side on a baking sheet and sprinkle the tops generously with the remaining bread crumbs, pressing them in gently to adhere. (The shrimp can be prepared to this point up to 4 hours ahead, covered and refrigerated.)

4. Position a rack in the top third of the oven and preheat the oven to 425°F. Arrange the shrimp in a lightly oiled 15-by-10-inch baking dish. Pour the wine around the shrimp. Drizzle the tops of the shrimp with the oil. Bake until the shrimp turn opaque, 12 to 15 minutes.

5. Transfer 3 shrimp to each dinner plate. Whisk the remaining 2 tablespoons butter into the wine in the baking dish. Pour equal amounts of the wine mixture over each serving. Sprinkle with the parsley, add the lemon wedges, and serve hot.

LOBSTER NEWBERG

Lobster Newberg had been on Manhattan menus for over seventy-five years when it made a midcentury comeback, partly due to its pyrotechnical pleasures, and also because it can be made with a minimum of ingredients. But fair warning: Newberg is costly to make unless you have a lobster trap next to your yacht. It is often served in pastry shells to help stretch the portions, which we have done here. You can also experiment by substituting less expensive shrimp or scallops for some of the lobster, or adding sautéed mushrooms to the finished dish. We do recommend that you make it with a chafing dish for that extra dash of *savoir faire*.

3 lobsters, cooked and cooled
2 tablespoons unsalted butter
3 tablespoons Cognac or brandy
2 tablespoons Madeira (California Madeira is fine.)
1¼ cups heavy cream
2 large egg yolks
Salt and ground hot red (cayenne) pepper
4 frozen puff pastry shells, baked according to package directions

1. Remove the lobster meat from the shells, reserving any red roe and crumbling it to separate the tiny eggs. Discard the shells and viscera. Cut the meat into bite-sized pieces. You should have about 3½ cups meat.

2. In a large skillet melt the butter over medium heat. Add the lobster and cook, stirring often, just to heat the lobster through, about 1 minute. Use a slotted spoon to transfer the lobster to a small bowl. (If using a chafing dish, remove the water pan from the chafing dish holder. Cook the lobster in the skillet on the stove with the butter as directed above. Then bring the lobster in the skillet with the other ingredients to the dinner table. Ignite the chafing dish fuel and continue cooking.)

3. Pour the Cognac and Madeira into the skillet and heat over low heat until the liquors are beginning to simmer. Carefully ignite the liquors with a long match. Let them burn out of their own accord, or cover with the lid after 30 seconds.

4. Add the heavy cream and bring to a simmer over medium heat. Whisk the egg yolks in a small bowl. Ladle in about ½ cup of the hot cream mixture, whisk well, then whisk into the skillet. Add any reserved roe. Cook just until the sauce thickens without boiling, about 30 seconds. Do not overheat or the sauce will be grainy.

Remove from the heat and season with salt and hot pepper. Return the lobster to the skillet and stir well.

5. For each serving, place a pastry shell on a dinner plate, and spoon in the lobster mixture. Serve hot.

How to Succeed in Cooking Lobster

Most fish stores will cook the lobster for you—so let them! If you have to cook the lobsters yourself, it is easy to do, as long as you have nerves of steel.

Try to cook the lobsters immediately after bringing them home from the market. If you refrigerate them, poke holes in the bag so they don't suffocate. Bring a very large pot of salted water to a boil over high heat. There will probably be only enough room in the pot to cook one lobster at a time. Plunge the live lobster head first into the water. Cover and cook until the lobster shell has turned deep red, about 15 minutes. Use tongs to remove the lobster from the water. Transfer to a bowl of iced water to cool.

Not your scene? Broil 5 lobster tails, brushed with melted butter, about 8 inches from the source of heat, until the meat is opaque, about 8 minutes. Remove the meat from the shells, chop it up, and you are ready to Newberg-ize the lobster.

The Name Game

Like many well-known dishes, Lobster Newberg was named for the person who invented it. Well, sort of . . . The dish was originated by Ben Wenberg, a patron at celebrity hangout Delmonico's in the 1870s, and "Lobster Wenberg" ended up on the menu. When restaurant owner and customer had a falling-out, the dish was renamed *New*berg. Banana-fana fo unfair!

MATTERHORN FONDUE

In the early Sixties, the biggest attraction in the country was Disneyland's Matterhorn Bobsleds ride. The 147-foot-high attraction—a true $^1/_{100}$th scale replica of the actual mountain in Switzerland—loomed large in both fun and food culture. By the mid-Sixties, fondue was a hit at home and in restaurants. Dating back to seventeenth century Switzerland, fondue is technically a mix of different cheese, wine, and seasonings melted and served in a communal pot. Today, there are all kinds of heated sauces that share the same name, including savory, fruit, and chocolate choices.

2½ cups (9 ounces) shredded Gruyère cheese
2½ cups (9 ounces) shredded Emmentaler cheese
½ cup (3 ounces), ½-inch diced Appenzeller cheese
4 teaspoons cornstarch
1 garlic clove, peeled
1 cup dry white wine (see Stick a Fork in It: Fondue Tips on opposite page)
1 tablespoon fresh lemon juice
1 tablespoon kirsch, Cognac, or brandy
A few gratings of fresh nutmeg
Freshly ground pepper, to taste

1. Toss the Gruyère, Emmentaler, and Appenzeller cheese with the cornstarch in a large bowl.

2. Rub the inside of a heavy-bottomed medium saucepan with the garlic; discard the garlic. Add the wine and lemon juice and bring to a bare simmer over medium heat.

3. A handful at a time, stir the cheese mixture into the wine, stirring the first batch until it is almost completely melted before adding another. The fondue can bubble gently, but do not boil. Stir in the kirsch and season with the nutmeg and pepper.

4. Transfer to a cheese fondue pot and keep warm over a fondue burner. Serve immediately, with dipping ingredients of your choice.

Stick a Fork in It: Fondue Tips

Fondue can be temperamental, unless you follow these tips.

- The fondue pot is really to keep the cooked fondue warm, and not meant for tableside cooking. Make the fondue in the kitchen, transfer to the pot, and then serve.
- The wine must be crisp and acidic, because if the wine is too soft, the cheese won't melt properly. Pinot grigio is a good choice; avoid chardonnay. The lemon adds a bit more acidity; substitute white wine vinegar, if you prefer.
- Don't let the fondue boil, or it will get grainy.
- Use all Gruyère, and skip the Emmentaler and Appenzeller, if you wish.
- When dipping the bread, drag it along the bottom of the pot to discourage the fondue from burning.

Swiss Secrets

The rise of Swiss food, particularly fondue, in the Sixties is another example of how international cuisine influenced American cooking. The classic cheese version first popped up on the American restaurant scene at Le Chalet Suisse in New York in 1956. It took off like an ignited Sterno, and by 1964, the restaurant's chef was asked to create a chocolate fondue with Toblerone chocolate. Although one can theorize about how the increase of European food products in the marketplace helped fuel the fad, we believe Walt Disney had something to do with it too.

Every Sunday night, before Ed Sullivan's variety hour, millions of people (and not just kids) tuned into Uncle Walt's extravaganza of a television show. Disneyland was heavily promoted on the show, and the theme park was home to the ultimate roller coaster in the country: the Matterhorn. A towering replica of the real mountain in Switzerland (and the scene of some tense moments in Disney's live-action film *Third Man on the Mountain*), with speeding toboggans racing through it, the first tubular steel roller coaster in the world was the Holy Grail of rides. Since cross-country travel was rare at the time, most kids could only dream of visiting the modern marvel. Did the Swiss food craze start because families had to make do with fondue? We say *ja*.

Random Disneyland trivia: one of us—we won't say who—was actually a plaid-skirted tour guide at Disneyland back in the day, so we can confirm the rumors are true: there is actually a basketball court inside the top of the Matterhorn.

"DON'T MESS WITH MOM" TUNA AND NOODLE CASSEROLE

MAKES 6 SERVINGS

Sometimes, you just can't mess with Mom. We considered updating this recipe, until we tasted the original, and were overcome by a pimiento-studded wave of childhood memories. This casserole was so easy to make it became a staple in many households, especially on Fridays during Lent.

Softened butter, for the casserole
6 cups (8 ounces) medium egg noodles
1 (10.75-ounce) can condensed cream of mushroom soup
¾ cup milk
2 (6-ounce) cans chunk tuna, drained and flaked
1 cup frozen peas, placed in a sieve and rinsed under hot water to lightly thaw
2 tablespoons drained and chopped pimiento (optional)
¾ cup crushed potato chips or croutons

1. Position a rack in the center of the oven and preheat the oven to 350°F. Lightly butter a 1½-quart casserole or baking dish.

2. Bring a large saucepan of salted water to a boil over high heat. Add the noodles and cook according to the package directions until almost tender. Remember, the noodles are going to be baked, so don't overcook them. Drain and return to the saucepan.

3. Add the soup, milk, tuna, peas, and pimiento, if using, and stir well. Transfer to the casserole and top with the potato chips.

4. Bake until the edges are bubbling, about 25 minutes. Let stand 5 minutes, then serve hot.

CHILE RELLENOS CASSEROLE

California cuisine was finding its footing in the Sixties, particularly with the introduction of Mexican influences into American food culture. Traditional *chile rellenos*—stuffed, battered, and deep-fried—is not the easiest of entrées to make for a party, unless you transform them into the oh-so-Sixties casserole form, as we've done here. This ultra-California dish is best enjoyed to the strains of the Beach Boys. A Malibu setting is entirely optional.

Softened butter, for the baking dish
3 (7-ounce) cans of green chiles, split lengthwise
2 cups (8 ounces) shredded sharp Cheddar cheese or Mexican cheese mix; divided
5 large eggs
1¼ cups half-and-half
3 tablespoons all-purpose flour
1¾ teaspoons baking powder
¼ teaspoon salt
1 (8-ounce) can tomato sauce
1 tablespoon chili powder

1. Position a rack in the center of the oven and preheat the oven to 350ºF. Butter a 13-by-9-inch baking dish.

2. Spread half of the chiles in the baking dish and sprinkle with 1 cup of cheese. Top with the remaining chiles. Whisk the eggs, half-and-half, flour, baking powder, and salt together in a medium bowl to dissolve the flour. Pour into the baking dish.

3. Bake until the egg mixture is puffed and beginning to brown, about 30 minutes. Mix the tomato sauce and chili powder in a small bowl. Spread over the egg mixture and sprinkle with the remaining 1 cup cheese. Continue baking until the cheese melts, about 5 minutes longer.

4. Let stand 5 minutes, then serve hot.

CHAPTER 5
BEST SUPPORTING PLAYERS: VEGETABLES AND SIDE DISHES

I n the Sixties, vegetables were often relegated to the background, not because of a national aversion, but limited local availability.

In a world full of exotic and organic fruits and vegetables, it's easy to forget it wasn't always that way. Before jet planes delivered blueberries from Chile to the neighborhood market in February, there could be a pretty long wait between fall and spring for fresh produce. In the meantime, potatoes, carrots, and their rather bland relatives had to do. This is why frozen veggies were such a food revolution—before that, home cooks had even less choice and were limited to their local farms, seasonal crops, and good harvests.

While the midcentury choices were basic compared to today, creative Sixties cooks often added cream sauces (and even more often, in the form of canned soup) to add a little oomph. Here are some of the best vegetable and side dishes of the era—proof that many moms did more than just spread cream cheese or peanut butter on celery sticks, sprinkle them with raisins, and call it a day (although on the days she did, we didn't complain).

ASPARAGUS AUX BLENDER HOLLANDAISE

Like many other French dishes that found their way into American homes, there is a time-saving twist that steers it away from *la tradition Française*. In this case, it's the blender, that magical appliance that does so much more than just make Daiquiris. Instead of painstakingly whisking the butter into the yolks drop-by-drop, you can whirl up a sauce in a minute or so.

HOLLANDAISE SAUCE

4 large egg yolks, preferably from pasteurized eggs (see Note)
1 tablespoon fresh lemon juice
¼ teaspoon kosher salt
⅛ teaspoon freshly ground white pepper
8 tablespoons (1 stick) unsalted butter

1 pound asparagus, woody stems trimmed

1. To make the hollandaise sauce, in a blender, combine the egg yolks, 1 tablespoon water, the lemon juice, salt, and white pepper. In a small saucepan, melt the butter over medium heat. With the blender running, slowly add the warm melted butter through the vent in the lid, processing until the sauce is thick and smooth. Taste and adjust the seasoning. If the sauce is too thick, add a bit more water to thin it. Transfer the sauce to a heatproof bowl. Cover and place over (but not in) a saucepan of hot, not simmering, water to keep warm. (The sauce is not supposed to be piping hot. The residual heat from the asparagus will sufficiently warm it.)

2. Bring a large pot of salted water to a boil over high heat. Add the asparagus and cook until barely tender, about 5 minutes, depending on the thickness of the asparagus. Drain well.

3. Transfer the asparagus to a serving platter. Spoon some of the hollandaise sauce on top, and transfer the remaining sauce to a small serving bowl. Serve at once.

NOTE: This recipe uses raw eggs, which have been known to carry the potentially harmful salmonella bacterium. Pasteurized eggs, available at some supermarkets, are safe to use. If you use standard eggs, do not serve this to the very young, elderly, or infirm people with compromised immune systems.

CREAMED CORN

How did this lush dish fall out of fashion? Let's not talk about fat grams, let's talk about flavor. Make it with summer corn, serve at a backyard barbeque, and sit back and wait for the moans to start. Or try it with fried chicken. Actually, there are many main courses it could enhance. Let's take this dish back from the babies. In Sixties-sized portions, it's well worth the calories.

5 ears fresh corn, husked
2 tablespoons unsalted butter
½ cup finely chopped yellow onion
2 tablespoons all-purpose flour
1¼ cups heavy cream, heated
Salt and freshly ground black pepper

1. One at a time, stand an ear of corn on its wide end (cut off the end so the ear doesn't rock, if needed). Run a large knife down the cob to cut off the kernels. Scrape the blade of the knife along the cob to release the "milk" (the juices and corn germ). You should have 4½ cups kernels and milk.

2. Heat the butter in a medium saucepan over medium heat. Add the onion and cook, stirring often, until softened, about 3 minutes. Sprinkle with the flour and stir well. Whisk in the cream and cook, whisking often, until simmering and thickened. Stir in the corn. Cook, stirring often, until the corn is heated through and tender, about 10 minutes. Season with salt and pepper. Serve hot.

KITCHEN TIME MACHINE

This dish is best with fresh corn. However, you can substitute 2 (10-ounce) boxes of corn kernels, thawed, for the fresh corn.

Flash Frozen

Clarence Birdseye wasn't the first person to freeze food for consumers. He was the first person to get it right. While working in the fur trade in northern Canada in 1912, he observed how Eskimos used ice, wind, and temperature to instantly freeze the fish they caught. The process of rapid freezing at extremely low temperatures didn't damage the cell walls of the food, meaning when they were defrosted, they kept their color, texture, and most importantly, taste.

He returned to the United States and invented a machine for quick freezing. It worked, and his family was one of the few with cabbage in the winter. But he was a little ahead of his time. While he rolled out a line of frozen vegetables and fish in 1930, not many Americans had freezers in their homes. When they finally got them, they were wary of Birdseye's "flash frozen" technique, as other conventionally frozen foods did not hold up well through the thaw. Birdseye persisted, collecting nearly 300 patents during his life. By the 1960s when America finally caught up to Birdseye's vision, he had sold the company that bore his name, and it became a market leader. Birds Eye, now owned by Pinnacle Foods, still flash freezes their products to this day.

Random trivia: Family legend says that the Birdseye name was given to the family by an English Queen when an early ancestor saved her life by shooting an attacking hawk in the eye.

GREEN BEANS IN MUSHROOM SAUCE

MAKES 6 SERVINGS

By the early Sixties, the green bean casserole made with frozen green beans, a can of mushroom soup, and French fried onions was already an iconic dish—a must-have at holiday meals. Here is a restaurant-quality from-scratch version with fresh green beans and mushrooms, with the classic recipe following.

GREEN BEANS

1 pound green beans, trimmed and cut into 1-inch lengths
2 tablespoons unsalted butter
½ cup finely chopped yellow onion
10 ounces white mushrooms, thinly sliced
2 tablespoons all-purpose flour
1 ½ cups whole milk
1 teaspoon soy sauce
Salt and freshly ground black pepper

ONION RINGS

Vegetable oil, for deep-frying
1 medium onion, cut into ⅛-inch-thick rounds and separated into rings
½ cup all-purpose flour
Salt and freshly ground black pepper

1. Bring a large pot of salted water to a boil over high heat. Add the green beans and cook until crisp-tender, about 4 minutes. Drain, rinse under cold running water, and drain well. (The green beans can be made up to 1 day ahead, cooled, wrapped in paper towels, and refrigerated in a plastic storage bag.)

2. Melt the butter in a large saucepan over medium heat. Add the onion and cook, stirring occasionally, until softened, about 3 minutes. Add the mushrooms and cook, stirring occasionally, until their juices evaporate and they are beginning to brown, about 8 minutes. Sprinkle with flour and stir well. Whisk in the milk. Cook, whisking often, until simmering and thickened. Reduce the heat to low and simmer, stirring often, until no raw flour taste remains, about 5 minutes. Stir in the soy sauce. Season with salt and pepper. (The sauce can be made up to 2 hours ahead, stored at room temperature. Reheat before using.)

3. Add the green beans and bring to a simmer. Cook until the green beans are heated through, about 3 minutes. Transfer to a serving bowl and cover to keep warm.

4. Meanwhile, pour enough oil to come halfway up the sides of a large, heavy (preferably cast-iron) skillet. Heat over high heat until the oil is shimmering or reads 350°F on a deep-frying thermometer. Line a baking sheet with brown paper.

5. In batches without crowding, toss the onions in flour and shake off the excess flour. Add to the oil and cook until golden brown, about 1½ minutes. Use a wire spider or slotted spoon to transfer to the paper to drain. Season the onion rings with salt and pepper.

6. Place the onion rings on the green beans and serve hot.

KITCHEN TIME MACHINE

For the classic "can of soup" Green Bean Casserole, mix 1 (10.75-ounce) can cream of mushroom soup, 1/2 cup milk, 1 teaspoon soy sauce, and a dash of freshly ground black pepper in a 1 1/2-quart casserole. Stir in 2 (10-ounce) boxes of frozen cut green beans, thawed, and half of a 2.8-ounce can of French fried onions. Bake in a preheated 350°F oven until bubbling, about 25 minutes. Stir and top with the remaining onions. Bake 5 minutes more. Makes 6 to 8 servings.

NOT-FROM-A-BOX MACARONI AND CHEESE

MAKES 4 TO 6 SERVINGS

. . . .

Raise your hand if you *didn't* glue macaroni to something in elementary school. Yeah, we didn't think so. There's something decidedly magical about macaroni in the classroom . . . and the kitchen. Whether the kids are climbing the walls or you're just in from a night on the town, boxed mac 'n' cheese is a blessing. But if you want to taste the best homemade macaroni and cheese you've ever had, try this Sixties baked cheesy macaroni casserole. Feel free to add tomato slices to the top.

4 tablespoons unsalted butter, divided, plus more for the casserole
8 ounces (2 cups) elbow macaroni or other twisty pasta
3 tablespoons all-purpose flour
2 cups whole milk, heated
8 ounces (2 cups) shredded sharp Cheddar cheese
½ teaspoon dry mustard
Salt and freshly ground black pepper
½ cup fresh bread crumbs

1. Position a rack in the center of the oven and preheat the oven to 350°F. Lightly butter a 1½-quart casserole.

2. Bring a large pot of salted water to a boil over high heat. Add the macaroni and cook according to the package directions until al dente. Drain well.

3. Return the pot to the stove. Add 3 tablespoons of butter and melt over medium-low heat. Add the flour and whisk until smooth. Let bubble for 1 minute without browning. Whisk in the milk and bring to a simmer, whisking often. Remove from the heat and add the cheese and dry mustard. Let stand for a minute or so, then whisk until the cheese is melted. Season with salt and pepper.

4. Transfer to the casserole. Sprinkle with the crumbs and dot with the remaining 1 tablespoon butter. Bake until bubbly and the top is golden brown, about 25 minutes. Let stand 5 minutes. Serve hot.

KITCHEN TIME MACHINE

For a milder macaroni and cheese, substitute 8 ounces of processed cheese product, such as Velveeta, for the Cheddar cheese, and use crushed saltine crackers instead of the bread crumbs.

A Mint Julep Jamboree

When you have a hankerin' for country music and fried chicken, this menu will go down nice and easy. A "Best Beehive Contest" would be a great added attraction.

Mint Juleps (page 193)
Lemonade

Pimiento and Walnut Cheese Ball (page 32)
Deviled Eggs (page 24)

Soulful Fried Chicken (page 100)
Creamed Corn (page 126)
Not-from-a-Box Macaroni and Cheese (page 130)
Sliced tomatoes with Red French Dressing (page 55)
Homemade Biscuits (page 139)

Southern Caramel Cake (page 155)
Coffee and tea
Southern Comfort

CD Playlist

Patsy Cline, *The Definitive Collection*
Various, *Classic Country 1960-1964*
Various, *Oh Brother, Where Art Thou? Soundtrack*

GRANDMOTHER'S NOODLES WITH SOUR CREAM AND POPPY SEEDS

Carb counting was not a fad in the Sixties, as evidenced by the popularity of creamy sauces served over pasta as a side dish. This classic midcentury noodle recipe, which sometimes goes by the name Noodles Romanoff, is decidedly European and positively delicious. Sitting on a phone book while eating it is not required, but it will help conjure up memories of Grandmother's house.

8 ounces wide egg noodles
2 tablespoons unsalted butter
½ cup chopped yellow onion
2 tablespoons poppy seeds
½ cup sour cream, at room temperature
Salt and freshly ground black pepper

1. Bring a large saucepan of lightly salted water to a boil over high heat. Add the noodles and cook according to the package directions until tender. Drain, rinse under cold running water, and drain well.

2. Meanwhile, melt the butter in a large skillet over medium heat. Add the onion and cook, stirring occasionally, until translucent, about 5 minutes. Stir in the poppy seeds. Add the noodles and cook until heated through, about 1 minute. Reduce the heat to low. Add the sour cream and stir until melted and hot, but not boiling, about 1 minute more. Season with salt and pepper. Serve hot.

POTATOES AU GRATIN

These scalloped potatoes are just the thing to serve with baked ham or meat loaf. But, set aside a good chunk of time to bake the potatoes into creamy, tender submission. Parboiling them before baking helps—skip this step, and the potatoes could take two hours to cook.

3 pounds baking (russet or Burbank) potatoes, peeled and cut into ¼-inch rounds
4 tablespoons (½ stick) unsalted butter, plus more for the baking dish
¼ cup all-purpose flour
2½ cups whole milk, heated
2 cups (8 ounces) shredded sharp Cheddar cheese, divided
Salt and freshly ground black pepper
½ cup chopped yellow onion

1. Position a rack in the center of the oven and preheat the oven to 350°F. Lightly butter a 13-by-9-inch baking dish.

2. Bring a large pot of salted water to a boil over high heat. Add the potatoes and cook until they are beginning to soften, about 5 minutes. Drain.

3. Melt the butter in a medium saucepan over medium-low heat. Whisk in the flour. Let bubble without browning for 1 minute. Whisk in the milk. Cook, whisking often, until the sauce is simmering and thickened. Remove from the heat and stir in 1½ cups of the Cheddar cheese. Season with salt and pepper.

4. Spread half of the potatoes in the baking dish. Pour in half of the sauce, spread evenly, and sprinkle with the onions. Repeat with the remaining onions and sauce.

5. Bake until the potatoes are tender, about 1½ hours. Sprinkle the top with the remaining ½ cup Cheddar cheese, and continue baking until the cheese melts, about 5 minutes more. Let stand 10 minutes, then serve hot.

BUTTER-WHIPPED POTATOES

You can mash potatoes with a masher, or you can whip them with a mixer. In the appliance-crazy Sixties, the mixer makes fun out of a chore, and you'll get fluffy, smooth potatoes for the minimal effort. Yes, there is an entire stick of butter in these potatoes, but that is just the secret that will have everyone asking for the recipe.

3 pounds baking (russet or Burbank) potatoes, peeled and cut into 1½-inch chunks
½ cup (1 stick) unsalted butter, at room temperature
½ cup whole milk, heated
Salt and freshly ground black pepper

1. Bring a large saucepan of salted water to a boil over high heat. Add the potatoes and partially cover the pot. Reduce the heat to medium. Cook the potatoes at a serious simmer until tender, about 25 minutes. Drain well.

2. Return the drained potatoes to the saucepan. Cook over low heat, stirring continuously, to lightly dry and release excess steam from the potatoes, about 2 minutes. Remove from the heat.

3. Using an electric mixer, whip the potatoes on high speed, adding the butter and milk, until smooth. Season with salt and pepper. Serve hot.

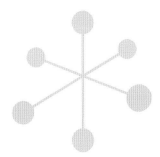

STEAKHOUSE CREAMED SPINACH

In the Sixties, as now, one of the favorite places for business people and celebrating couples to dine was a steakhouse. At these establishments, the side dishes are as important as the meat. Creamed spinach is such a dish. Here's a home version that's sure to impress dedicated carnivores.

3 (9-ounce) bags fresh spinach, tough stems removed, well-rinsed but not dried
1 cup canned reduced-sodium chicken broth
¾ cup heavy cream
3 tablespoons unsalted butter
1 garlic clove, crushed through a press
3 tablespoons all-purpose flour
A few gratings of fresh nutmeg
Salt and freshly ground pepper

1. Bring 1 cup lightly salted water to a boil in a large saucepan over high heat. In batches, add the spinach, stirring until the first batch is wilted before adding the next. Cover tightly and reduce the heat to medium. Cook until the spinach is tender, about 5 minutes.

2. Drain the spinach over a bowl, reserving 1¼ cups of the cooking water. Rinse the spinach under cold water. A handful at a time, squeeze the spinach between your fingers to remove excess water and to "chop" the spinach. Transfer to a bowl.

3. Heat the reserved cooking water, broth, and heavy cream in a medium saucepan until simmering. Heat the butter and garlic in a medium saucepan over medium-low heat, just until the butter melts. Whisk in the flour and let bubble without browning for 2 minutes. Whisk in the hot cream mixture and bring to a simmer. Cook, whisking often, until the sauce is thickened and no raw flour taste remains, about 5 minutes. Stir in the spinach. Season with the nutmeg, salt, and pepper. Transfer to a serving bowl and serve hot.

KITCHEN TIME MACHINE

Substitute 3 (10-ounce) boxes frozen chopped spinach, thawed and squeezed dry, for the freshly cooked spinach.

CANDIED YAMS WITH MARSHMALLOW TOPPING

MAKES 8 SERVINGS

We're not gonna lie. When we were kids, we were not huge fans of canned candied yams (call them sweet potatoes, if you wish). However, fresh yams are another situation altogether, even if the dish is still candy-sweet. Be careful when adding the marshmallows, though, as they tend to melt completely if they come in contact with liquid. If the yams seem too syrupy, remove some of the cooking liquid with a bulb baster.

3½ pounds orange-fleshed yams (sweet potatoes), peeled and cut into ¼-inch rounds
½ cup packed light or dark brown sugar
4 tablespoons (½ stick) unsalted butter, cut into small cubes, plus more for the baking dish
1 (10.5-ounce) bag mini marshmallows

1. Position a rack in the center of the oven and preheat the oven to 400°F. Lightly butter a 13-by-9-inch baking dish.

2. Bring a large saucepan of salted water to a boil over high heat. Add the yams, cover, and return to a boil. Cook until they are beginning to soften, about 5 minutes. Drain well. Spread the yams in the dish, sprinkle with the brown sugar, and dot with the butter. Cover the dish with aluminum foil.

3. Bake until the yams are tender, about 30 minutes. Remove from the oven. If the yams seem soupy, remove some of the syrup with a bulb baster. Position the rack about 6 inches from the source of heat and preheat the broiler.

4. Sprinkle the marshmallows over the yams. Broil just until the marshmallows are lightly browned, about 3 minutes. Serve hot.

KITCHEN TIME MACHINE

Substitute 1 (40-ounce) can candied yams in syrup for the freshly prepared yams. Sprinkle with the brown sugar, dot with the butter, and bake and top as directed in the recipe.

EVERYONE LOVES IT STUFFING

Here's a basic stuffing that every member of the family is bound to enjoy—unless someone likes oyster stuffing, and then they have to fend for themselves. Stuffing food into meat cavities has been around as a written recipe since Roman times (although the prim Victorians adopted the less scandalous moniker of "dressing"). To make history with your bird, always use warm, freshly prepared stuffing so it is likely to cook to the safe eating temperature of 160°F, something that may not happen if the stuffing is made ahead and refrigerated. You will always have leftover stuffing, as it all cannot fit inside of the fowl, so bake it in a shallow casserole as a side dish.

1 pound firm white sandwich bread, cut into ½-inch cubes (10 cups)
8 tablespoons (1 stick) unsalted butter
1 large onion, chopped
3 medium celery ribs with leaves, chopped
¼ cup chopped fresh parsley
3 cups canned reduced-sodium chicken broth or homemade turkey stock (see the stock made from the turkey giblets on page 109), as needed
2 teaspoons poultry seasoning
Salt and freshly ground black pepper

1. The night before making the stuffing, spread the bread cubes out on baking sheets. Let stand at room temperature, uncovered, to dry and stale.

2. The next day, melt the butter in a large skillet over medium heat. Add the onion and celery and cover. Cook, stirring often, until the onion is golden, about 10 minutes.

3. Scrape the vegetables and butter into a large bowl. Add the bread cubes and parsley. Stir in enough of the broth to moisten the stuffing, about 2½ cups. Season with the poultry seasoning. Use to stuff the turkey, or place in a buttered baking dish, drizzle with an additional ½ cup broth, cover, and bake as a side dish.

KITCHEN TIME MACHINE

Substitute 1 (14-ounce) bag bread stuffing cubes (seasoned or plain) for the cubed bread.

HOMEMADE BISCUITS

There is nothing like the aroma of freshly baked biscuits to smooth the edges of a frazzled day. You can make your biscuits from a mix, with shortening instead of lard, with regular milk, with standard flour . . . or you can make them extra special. Here we share the little Southern tricks that make all the difference. Freeze any leftovers to have on hand to toast for a quick breakfast or to serve with Chicken à la King (page 106).

1½ cups all-purpose flour
1½ cups cake flour (not self-rising)
2½ teaspoons baking powder
1 teaspoon baking soda
1 teaspoon salt
8 tablespoons chilled lard (see Note)
1 cup buttermilk, as needed

1. Position a rack in the center of the oven and preheat to 400°F.

2. Sift the flour, cake flour, baking powder, baking soda, and salt together into a medium bowl. Add the lard. Use a pastry blender to cut the lard into the flour mixture until the mixture resembles coarse bread crumbs with pea-sized pieces of lard. Stir in enough of the buttermilk to make a soft dough that cleans the sides of the bowl.

3. Dust a work surface with flour. Turn the dough out onto the work surface and knead a few times to smooth the dough. Pat the dough into a rectangle a little more than ¾ inch thick. Using a 2 ½-inch-diameter biscuit cutter, cut out the biscuits. Gather up the scraps, knead together very briefly, and pat and cut out more biscuits. Continue until all of the dough has been used. The key here is to handle the dough very lightly, especially when reusing the scraps, as overworked dough makes tough biscuits. (For rectangular biscuits, which do not require a biscuit cutter and do not create scraps, pat the dough into a 9-by-7-inch rectangle. Cut lengthwise into thirds, and crosswise into quarters, to make 12 rectangles.)

4. Arrange on an ungreased baking sheet. Bake until the biscuits have risen and are golden brown, about 20 minutes. Serve hot.

NOTE: You can substitute vegetable shortening for the lard. Or use unsalted butter, cut into ½-inch cubes. But we do declare, lard makes the flakiest, tastiest biscuits.

Fat . . . with Flavor

Paula Deen is right: everything tastes better with butter. And according to the Harvard School of Public Health, butter isn't as unhealthy as we've been led to believe.

While consuming large quantities of any fat isn't a great idea for optimum health, natural products like butter and its creamy white cousin lard are better choices than hydrogenated, chemically-created alternatives like margarine and shortening that contain trans fats. And while there are trans fat-free versions, the real issue is flavor. Have you ever tasted shortening? Enough said.

Or, give lard a try. The trick is to find minimally processed lard. Ask for it at privately owned butcher shops. They aren't as easy to find as they used to be, but there is a burgeoning artisan butcher movement going on, and there might be one in your vicinity. The meat vendors at many farmers' markets also now sell lard. When you make the Homemade Biscuits (page 139) with lard, you will be a convert. (But we do provide alternatives for those of you who are not pork eaters.)

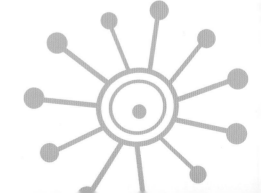

BUTTERMILK DINNER ROLLS

· · · · · · ·
MAKES 8 ROLLS
· · · · · · ·

Is there a kid that doesn't love fresh dinner rolls more than anything else on the table? Is there an adult? Try an unscientific test at your dinner table with these feather-light homemade rolls. Buttermilk is the secret weapon of many a great baker, and it's what elevates this divine bread. Its tangy acidity works to tenderize the flour, reacts with baking soda for a lively rise, and adds flavor too.

1 (¼-ounce) envelope active dry yeast (see Note on opposite page)
2 tablespoons warm (105°F to 115°F) water
3 tablespoons unsalted butter, plus more for the baking pan
¾ cup buttermilk
1 teaspoon sugar
1 teaspoon salt
¾ teaspoon baking soda
2⅔ cups all-purpose flour, as needed

1. Sprinkle the yeast over the warm water in a small bowl. Let stand until the yeast softens, about 5 minutes. Stir to dissolve the yeast.

2. Melt the butter in a small saucepan over low heat. Add the buttermilk and remove from the heat. Let stand, stirring often, until the buttermilk feels lukewarm to the touch, about 2 minutes. Pour into a large bowl. Add the sugar, salt, and baking soda and stir to combine. Gradually stir in enough of the flour to make a soft dough. Flour the work surface. Turn the dough out onto the work surface and knead, adding more of the flour as necessary (if the dough is tacky, but not sticking to the work surface, you have enough flour), to make a smooth, supple dough, about 6 minutes.

To make with a heavy-duty standing mixer, pour the buttermilk mixture into the work bowl. Add the sugar, salt, and baking soda. Mix with the paddle attachment on low speed. Gradually add enough flour to make a dough that cleans the sides of the bowl. Change the paddle attachment to the dough hook. Knead on medium-low speed, adding more flour as necessary, until the dough is smooth and supple, about 6 minutes.

3. Lightly butter a medium bowl. Shape the dough into a ball, place in the bowl, and rotate the dough to coat with butter. Cover with plastic wrap. Let stand in a warm, draft-free place until doubled in volume (if you poke a finger into the dough, the impression will remain for at least 5 seconds before filling in), about 1¼ hours.

4. Punch down the dough. Turn out onto the work surface. Cut into 8 equal portions. Shape each portion into a ball. Butter a 9-inch-diameter cake pan. Place the balls in the pan, with 1 ball in the center and the others spaced evenly around it. Cover with the plastic wrap and let stand until almost doubled, about 45 minutes.

5. Position a rack in the center of the oven and preheat to 350ºF. Uncover the rolls and bake until golden brown, about 20 minutes. Brush the tops of the rolls with softened butter. Let stand in the pan for 5 minutes. Remove the rolls from the pan and serve hot.

NOTE: If you are the kind of person who never bakes with yeast because you are afraid of taking the water's temperature, take heart. Use quick-rising (bread machine or instant) yeast, and you won't have to worry about the temperature, as this yeast works in cold water. Reduce the yeast to 2 teaspoons, and add it to 2 tablespoons cold (not warm) water.

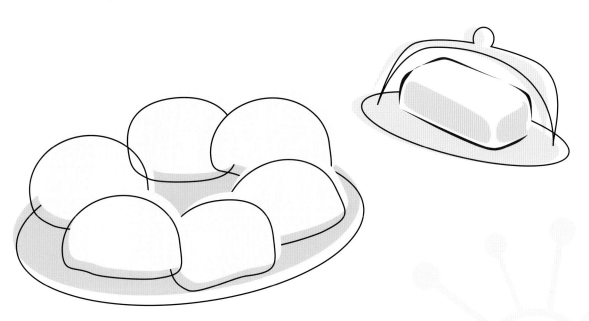

CHAPTER 6
SHOWSTOPPERS: DESSERTS

◇◇◇

Yet another reason why we love the Sixties—dinner always came with dessert. Even if it was only a little ramekin of fruit cocktail or a Sara Lee cake from the freezer, you could expect a happy ending.

Desserts in the Sixties were colorful, over-the-top, and usually on fire. The Moors have been igniting their food since the fourteenth century, but the practice didn't really catch on in America until the 1950s and '60s. It became an easy way to end your dinner party with a bang. Popular flaming desserts included baked Alaska, crêpes Suzette, cherries jubilee, and pretty much anything you squirted 80 proof rum over.

If the dessert didn't have liquor on it, then there was often booze in it. No one thought twice about serving grasshopper pie, with its high crème de menthe content, to kids. There are plenty of desserts here that don't require a photo ID, and we also give tips on how to cook without alcohol on page 169. In some cases, the booze is the dessert's *raison d'être*, so if you don't want to cook with hooch, make something else.

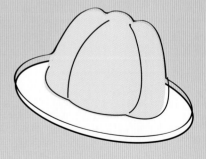

Flambé

The actual term for igniting warmed alcohol over food is *flambé* or "flamed" in French. Some chefs argue it creates a chemical reaction that changes the flavor of food, while others dismiss it as pure showmanship. In either case, we're in!

High Spirited Desserts

Not all desserts included alcohol just for show. Some used it for fun. Or to sell more product. In the mid-twentieth century, Knox Unflavored Gelatine and Heublein Cordials copublished a collection of "high spirited desserts" to encourage the use of their products together. The pamphlet suggested that if a cook adopted a "devil-may-care attitude" toward baking with booze, dinner guests would "click their heels with glee over a superb dessert." When they weren't falling into it, we're guessing.

TIP TOE INN'S LATTICE-TOPPED CHERRY CHEESECAKE

When Rick moved to Manhattan, his first restaurant job was on the Upper West Side. Whenever he served cheesecake to customers of a certain age, they would shake their heads and mutter, "It's good, but not as good as Tip Toe Inn's," a famous Jewish delicatessen that had been shuttered for years—even then. By a strange twist of fate, he later worked with Sarabeth Levine, one of New York's best bakers . . . and a member of the family that owned the Tip Toe. While the small, nondescript restaurant was far from the madding Midtown crowd, its cherry cheesecake attracted patrons from all over the city. What made theirs tops in a city known for the creamy dessert? A delectable sugar cookie lattice crust. Master this recipe, and people will start crossing your town to feast on it.

SUGAR COOKIE DOUGH CRUST

1½ cups all-purpose flour
½ teaspoon baking powder
¼ teaspoon salt
7 tablespoons (1 stick minus 1 tablespoon) unsalted butter, chilled, cut into ½-inch cubes
⅓ cup sugar
1 large egg yolk
1 tablespoon sour cream
1 teaspoon vanilla extract

1 large egg, beaten, for glazing

FILLING

2 pounds cream cheese, softened at room temperature for at least 2 hours
1 cup sugar
¾ cup sour cream
4 large eggs, at room temperature, beaten
2 tablespoons cornstarch
1 teaspoon vanilla extract

2 teaspoons all-purpose flour, for dusting cookie dough
1 (21-ounce) can cherry pie filling

1. To make the cookie dough, sift the flour, baking powder, and salt together. Cream the butter and sugar with an electric mixer on high speed until light in color and texture, about 3 minutes. Beat in the egg yolk, sour cream, and vanilla. With the mixer on low speed, gradually beat in the flour mixture, just until it clumps together.

2. Divide the dough in half. Shape each portion into a thick disk, wrap in plastic wrap, and refrigerate just until chilled and firm enough to roll out, about 30 minutes.

3. Position a rack in the center of the oven and preheat to 350°F. Lightly butter a 9-inch springform pan. Line a baking sheet with parchment paper.

4. Lightly flour the work surface. Roll out 1 dough disk (keep the remaining dough refrigerated) into a 10-inch-diameter round about ⅛ inch thick. Using the bottom of the springform pan as a template, cut out the dough into a 9-inch round, discarding the trimmings. Transfer the round to the lined baking sheet. Cover loosely with plastic wrap and refrigerate the dough round while baking the cheesecake.

5. Roll out the second dough disk into a 10-inch-diameter round about ⅛ inch thick, trim into a 9-inch round as before, and fit into the bottom of the springform pan. Pierce the dough all over with a fork. Bake until the crust is lightly browned, about 15 minutes. Remove from the oven.

6. Reduce the oven temperature to 325°F. Beat the cream cheese and sugar in a large bowl with an electric mixer on medium speed, scraping down the sides of the bowl often, just until smooth. Beat in the sour cream, then gradually beat in the eggs. Beat in the cornstarch and vanilla. Pour into the pan with the warm crust.

7. Return to the oven and bake until the sides of the cheesecake have risen slightly and are barely beginning to color (the center of the filling will still jiggle when the pan is gently shaken and look unset), about 45 minutes.

8. Transfer the cheesecake to a wire cake rack. Carefully run a thin, sharp knife around the inside of the pan. Let cool completely.

9. Meanwhile, to make the lattice topping, return the oven temperature to 350°F. Cover the dough on the baking sheet. Keeping the dough on the baking sheet, dust the top of the dough with the flour. Use the end of a ½-inch-wide plain pastry tip or an aspic cutter to punch a perforated design into the dough. Discard the trimmings. Using a sharp knife, score the lattice round into 10 or 12 wedges (depending on the size of cheesecake slices you want to serve), but do not cut through the dough or separate the wedges. Very lightly brush the top of the lattice with some of the beaten egg, being sure that the egg doesn't run down onto the parchment paper. Bake until the lattice is golden brown, about 10 to 12 minutes. Let cool on the baking sheet. Cover with plastic wrap.

10. Spread the cherry pie filling on top of the cheesecake and refrigerate until chilled and set, at least 2 hours or overnight. Run a sharp knife around the insides of the pan again, and remove the sides of the pan. Using a sharp knife, following the original scoring marks, cut the lattice into 10 or 12 wedges. Following their original sequence, place the lattice wedges on top of the cheesecake. Using a thin knife rinsed under hot water, cut into slices, keeping the wedges in place, and serve chilled.

NOTE: Professional bakeries like the Tip Toe Inn use a lattice cutter, a cylinder with raised tabs on a handle, to cut the pattern into the cookie dough. When the cylinder is rolled over the dough, it cuts slits that will open and form the lattice when the dough is stretched. This cutter is available at bakery supply stores and well-stocked kitchen supply shops. But as you will probably only use it for making this cheesecake, it isn't worth the money and extra clutter in your kitchen drawer. It is much easier to use some other kind of tool for cutting the pattern into the dough. A pastry tip or aspic cutter work well, but you could even use the end of an apple corer.

ROCKY ROAD CUPCAKES

A well-known candy bar and ice cream flavor for years, Rocky Road became a popular cake creation in the creative Sixties. We think the fantastic combination of chocolate, marshmallow, and nuts would be great in any form, any time, but it's practically perfect in every way for cupcakes.

CAKE

4 ounces unsweetened chocolate, finely chopped
1 cup full-fat sour cream, at room temperature
⅔ cup (about) water
1 teaspoon vanilla extract
2 cups cake flour (not self-rising)
2 cups sugar
½ cup (1 stick) unsalted butter, at very soft room temperature, plus softened butter for the pans
2 large eggs, at room temperature, beaten together
½ teaspoon baking powder
1 teaspoon baking soda
½ teaspoon salt

CHOCOLATE BUTTERCREAM

4 ounces unsweetened chocolate, finely chopped
1½ cups (3 sticks) unsalted butter, at room temperature
1 (7.5-ounce) jar marshmallow cream
½ teaspoon vanilla extract

1 cup mini marshmallows
¾ cup coarsely chopped walnuts

1. Position a rack in the center of the oven and preheat to 350°F. Line 18 standard muffin cups with paper liners.

2. In the top part of a double boiler over hot, not simmering, water, melt the chocolate. Remove from the heat and cool until tepid.

3. Whisk the sour cream with enough water to measure 1½ cups, and add the vanilla. Sift the cake flour, sugar, butter, eggs, baking powder, baking soda, and salt together. Beat the butter in a large bowl with an electric mixer on high speed until creamy, about 1 minute. Gradually beat in the sugar and beat, scraping down the sides of the bowl occasionally with a rubber spatula, until light in color and texture, about 3 minutes. Gradually beat in the eggs. With the mixer on low speed, add the flour mixture in thirds, alternating with two equal additions of the sour cream mixture, and mix, scraping down the sides of the bowl as needed, until smooth. Spoon equal amounts of the batter into the muffin cups (an ice-cream scoop works well), filling them about three-quarters full. Smooth the tops.

4. Bake until a wooden toothpick inserted in the center of a cupcake comes out clean, about 20 minutes. Transfer the pans to wire cake racks and cool for 10 minutes. Remove the cupcakes from the pans. Transfer to the racks and let cool completely.

5. To make the buttercream, melt the chocolate in the top part of a double boiler over very hot, but not simmering, water. Remove from the heat and let cool until tepid, but still fluid.

6. Beat the butter in a medium bowl with an electric mixer on high speed until completely smooth, about 1 minute. In four or five additions, gradually beat in the marshmallow cream. Beat in the vanilla. Beat in the cooled chocolate. Immediately spread the frosting over the cupcakes.

7. Mix the marshmallows and walnuts in a medium bowl. Working over a rimmed baking sheet, press handfuls of the mixture onto the frosting. (The cupcakes can be prepared up to 1 day ahead, loosely covered with plastic wrap and stored at room temperature. Refrigeration could soften the marshmallows.)

PINEAPPLE UPSIDE-DOWN CAKE

This all-American cake, with its jaunty rings of pineapple and splotches of red cherries, was popular long before Hawaii was admitted to statehood. It was the perfect dessert for a Sixties housewife, as she was expected to have all kinds of canned goods on hand for cooking at the last minute. Serve the cake warm with a scoop of vanilla ice cream.

TOPPING

6 tablespoons unsalted butter
1 cup packed light brown sugar
7 canned pineapple rings (from a 20-ounce can), drained
7 maraschino cherries, stemmed

CAKE

1½ cups all-purpose flour
1½ teaspoons baking powder
¼ teaspoon salt
½ cup (1 stick) unsalted butter, at room temperature
½ cup sugar
2 large eggs, beaten
1 teaspoon vanilla extract
½ cup whole milk

1. Position a rack in the center of the oven and preheat to 350°F.

2. To make the topping, melt the butter in a heavy gauge, 9-by-2-inch heavy cake pan (or a 9-inch cast-iron skillet) over medium heat. Sprinkle in the brown sugar and cook, stirring occasionally, until the sugar is melted. Remove from the heat. Carefully arrange the pineapple rings in the pan, with 1 ring in the center and the remaining rings around it, and place a cherry in the center of each ring. Set aside.

3. To make the cake, sift the flour, baking powder, and salt together. Beat the butter in a medium bowl with an electric mixer on high speed until creamy, about 1 minute. Gradually beat in the sugar, occasionally scraping down the sides of the bowl with a rubber spatula, and beat until the mixture is light in color and texture, about 3 minutes. Gradually beat in the eggs, then the vanilla. With the mixer on low speed, beat in the flour in thirds, alternating with two equal additions of the milk, scraping down the bowl as needed, and mix until smooth. Spread evenly in the pan.

4. Bake until the cake is golden brown and top springs back when pressed in the center with your finger, about 30 minutes. Let cool in the pan for 2 minutes. Run a dinner knife around the inside of the pan. Place a serving plate over the pan. Use a thick kitchen towel to hold the pan and plate together and give them a sharp shake. Lift up and remove the pan. If any of the filling remains in the pan, just use a fork to transfer it to the cake. Let cool for about 15 minutes. Serve the cake warm or cooled to room temperature.

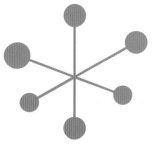

SOUTHERN CARAMEL CAKE

Based on a recipe from Rick's friend Martha Foose from her award-winning cookbook *Screen Doors and Sweet Tea*, where it is called Commitment Cake, this cake does take some commitment of time and attention. It is surely the dessert that Minny, a character in *The Help,* Kathryn Stockett's contemporary look at race relations in the Sixties, made for her loved ones. Don't make this on a rainy day, or the caramel frosting could act up and not set.

CAKE

2½ cups cake flour (not self-rising), plus more for the pan

1 tablespoon plus 1 teaspoon baking powder

1 teaspoon salt

1 cup whole milk

1 tablespoon vanilla extract

½ teaspoon almond extract (optional)

2 cups (4 sticks) unsalted butter, at room temperature, plus more for the pan

3 cups sugar

8 large eggs, at room temperature

CARAMEL FROSTING

2½ cups sugar

1 cup (2 sticks) unsalted butter, cut into tablespoons

¾ cup buttermilk

1 tablespoon plus 1 teaspoon light corn syrup

1¼ teaspoons baking soda

½ teaspoon salt

15 large marshmallows

1 tablespoon vanilla extract

1. To make the cake, position a rack in the center of the oven and preheat the oven to 350°F. Lightly butter two 9-inch round cake pans. Line the bottoms of the pans with rounds of waxed or parchment paper. Dust flour inside the pans to coat, and shake out the excess flour.

2. Sift the flour, baking powder, and salt together in a medium bowl. Stir the milk, vanilla, and almond extract, if using, in a glass measuring cup.

3. Beat the butter in a large bowl with an electric mixer on high speed until creamy, about 1 minute. Gradually beat in the sugar. Continue beating until the mixture is light in color and texture, about 3 minutes. One at a time, beat in the eggs, beating well after each addition. Reduce the mixer speed to low. In thirds, add the flour mixture, alternating with two equal additions of the milk mixture, and mix, scraping down the sides of the bowl with a rubber spatula as needed, just until smooth. Divide equally among the pans and smooth the tops.

4. Bake until a wooden toothpick inserted in the centers of the cakes comes out clean, about 30 minutes. Transfer to a wire cooling rack and let stand for 10 minutes. Invert and unmold the cakes onto cooling racks, remove the paper, and turn right side up to cool completely. When cooled, use a long serrated knife to slice each cake in half horizontally to make 4 cake layers.

5. To make the frosting, combine the sugar, butter, buttermilk, corn syrup, baking soda, and salt together in a large, heavy-bottomed saucepan. Bring to a boil over high heat, stirring constantly until the sugar is dissolved. Add the marshmallows. Attach a candy thermometer to the pot. Cook, stirring often, until the mixture is beige and reaches 238°F (soft-ball stage) on the thermometer. Remove from the heat and stir in the vanilla.

6. Pour the sugar mixture into a heatproof bowl set on a wire cooling rack (this helps air circulate around the bowl so the mixture cools more quickly). Using an electric mixer set on high speed, beat until the mixture is cloudy, opaque, and spreadable, about 4 minutes. Place the bowl in a larger bowl of hot water to keep the frosting warm and spreadable. Working quickly, place a dab of frosting in the center of a serving plate. Place one cake layer on the plate. Spread with about ½ cup of the frosting. Repeat with the remaining layers. Spread the top and sides of the cake with the frosting. Let stand for at least 1 hour before serving. Slice and serve.

SOUSED GRASSHOPPER PIE

MAKES 8 SERVINGS

The Grasshopper Pie was inspired by the alcoholic drink of the same name (page 189) for its shared ingredients, flavor, and color. It's not a dessert to serve to kids, but for once you won't have to share.

CHOCOLATE CRUMB SHELL

1¼ cups crushed chocolate wafer or cookies

3 tablespoons sugar

4 tablespoons (½ stick) unsalted butter

FILLING

1 envelope (2 teaspoons) unflavored gelatin powder

3 large eggs, preferably from pasteurized eggs, separated (see Note on page 158)

½ cup sugar, divided

Pinch of salt

¼ cup green crème de menthe

2 tablespoons white crème de cacao

1 cup heavy cream

WHIPPED CREAM

½ cup heavy cream

1 tablespoon confectioners' sugar

½ teaspoon vanilla extract

8 chocolate-mint candies, such as Andes Thins, unwrapped

1. Position a rack in the center of the oven and preheat the oven to 350°F.

2. To make the crust, mix the chocolate wafer crumbs, sugar, and butter together in a small bowl. Press firmly and evenly into the bottom and up the sides of a 9-inch pie pan. Bake until the crust is set and smells sweet, about 10 minutes. Transfer to a wire cake rack and let cool completely.

3. To make the filling, sprinkle the gelatin over ½ cup of water in a small bowl. Let stand until the gelatin absorbs the water, about 5 minutes. Whisk the egg yolks, ¼ cup of sugar, and salt in a heatproof (preferably stainless steel) medium bowl. Add the soaked gelatin. Cook over a medium saucepan of simmering water, stirring constantly with a rubber spatula, until the gelatin is dissolved and the mixture is thick enough to coat the spatula (if you run your finger through the mixture on the spatula, it cuts a swath), about 4 minutes. Strain through a wire sieve into a medium bowl. Stir in the crème de menthe and crème de cacao. Place the bowl in a larger bowl of iced water. Let stand, stirring occasionally, until chilled and beginning to set, about 10 minutes.

4. Whip the egg whites in another medium bowl with an electric mixer on high speed until foamy. Gradually beat in the remaining ¼ cup sugar and beat until the whites are stiff and shiny, but not dry. Stir about one-quarter of the whites into the gelatin mixture, then fold in the remaining whites.

5. Whip the cream in chilled medium bowl. Stir about one-quarter of the whipped cream into the gelatin mixture, then fold in the remaining cream. Pour into the chocolate crust and smooth the top. Cover loosely with plastic wrap and refrigerate until chilled and set, at least 2 hours and up to 2 days.

6. To make the whipped cream, whip the cream, confectioners' sugar, and vanilla together in a chilled medium bowl with an electric mixer until the cream forms stiff peaks. Transfer the whipped cream to a pastry bag fitted with a ½-inch star tip. Pipe 8 equally placed cream rosettes around the perimeter of the filling. (Or spoon 8 dollops of cream around the filling.) Insert a mint in each rosette. Cut into 8 pieces, and serve chilled.

NOTE: This recipe uses raw eggs, which have been known to carry the potentially harmful salmonella bacterium. Pasteurized eggs, available at some supermarkets, are safe to use. If you use standard eggs, do not serve this to the very young, elderly, or infirm people with compromised immune systems.

BRANDY ALEXANDER PIE: Substitute 3 tablespoons brandy for the crème de menthe, and increase the crème de cacao to 3 tablespoons. Omit the chocolate mints. Decorate the top of the pie with chocolate shavings (see page 165).

KITCHEN TIME MACHINE

Omit the gelatin and water, eggs, sugar, and salt. Snip 30 large marshmallows into pieces with oiled kitchen scissors. Melt the marshmallows and ⅔ cup milk in the top part of a double boiler over simmering water, stirring often. (You can improvise a double boiler by placing a heatproof bowl over a saucepan of simmering water.) Let cool until tepid. Whisk in the liqueurs, then fold in the whipped cream. Pour into the chocolate crust.

Three-Martini Lunch

Don't forget to turn in your itemized expense account report after this party.

Martinis, Very Dry (page 194)

Iceberg Lettuce Wedge with Blue Cheese Dressing and Bacon (page 54)

Pan-Fried Steak with Butter (page 80) or grilled steak
Steakhouse Creamed Spinach (page 136)
Baked potatoes with sour cream and chives

French Bordeaux, as expensive and pretentious as possible

Soused Grasshopper Pie (page 157)
Coffee and tea
Cognac or brandy

CD PLayLiST

Frank Sinatra, *The Capitol Years*
Dean Martin, *Dino: The Essential Dean Martin*
Sammy Davis Jr., *That's All*

TART-TONGUED LEMON MERINGUE PIE

MAKES 8 SERVINGS

Lemon meringue pie has survived into our times, but if you order it at a restaurant, it is likely to be deconstructed somehow. We don't want a watered-down version: this *is* your mother or grandmother's puckery lemon meringue pie. One piece of advice: don't make lemon meringue pie on a rainy day, or the meringue will weep.

FILLING

8 large eggs
1⅔ cups sugar
3 tablespoons cornstarch
1 cup fresh lemon juice
¼ teaspoon salt
4 tablespoons (½ stick) unsalted butter
Grated zest of 3 lemons

Perfect Pie Dough (page 163), fully baked

MERINGUE

4 large egg whites (reserved from the filling), at room temperature
⅔ cup sugar
½ teaspoon vanilla extract

1. To make the filling, beat 4 eggs together in a small bowl. Separate the remaining 4 eggs, adding the yolks to the beaten eggs, and the whites to a large bowl. Cover the whites and let stand at room temperature.

2. Whisk the sugar and cornstarch together in a medium bowl. Add the beaten eggs and yolks and whisk again. Whisk in the lemon juice and salt. Transfer to a heavy-bottomed medium saucepan. Cook over medium heat, whisking almost constantly, until the filling comes to a full boil. Reduce the heat to low and cook for 30 seconds. Remove from the heat and whisk in the butter. Strain through a wire sieve into a bowl. Stir the zest into the filling. Pour the filling into the warm or cooled pie shell.

3. Immediately proceed to the meringue. Beat the reserved whites in a large bowl with an electric mixer set at high speed until the whites form soft peaks. Beat in the sugar, 1 tablespoon at a time, and beat until the meringue forms stiff, shiny peaks. Beat in the vanilla. Using a metal spatula, spread the meringue over the hot filling, being sure that the meringue touches the crust on all sides. (This helps keep the crust from shrinking.) Swirl the meringue with the spatula to form peaks.

4. Bake until the meringue is tinged with brown, about 5 minutes. Transfer to the cake rack and let cool completely, at least 3 hours.

5. To serve, cut into wedges with a sharp thin knife, dipping the knife into a glass of hot water between slices.

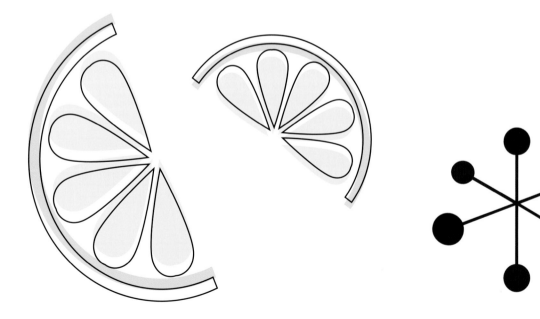

PERFECT PIE DOUGH

Then, as now, pie was the true test of the home baker's art, and even as the dessert repertoire has expanded, it remains an accomplishment to create a tender crust. The key ingredient to a reliably flaky crust is lard or vegetable shortening. This recipe adds butter for flavor and sugar to promote tenderness.

CRUST

1½ cups all-purpose flour, plus more for rolling out the dough
1 tablespoon sugar
¼ teaspoon salt
6 tablespoons chilled lard or vegetable shortening, and cut into ½-inch bits
2 tablespoons chilled unsalted butter, and cut into ½-inch cubes
⅓ cup iced water, as needed

1. To make the crust, stir the flour, sugar, and salt together in a medium bowl. Add the shortening and butter and stir to coat with flour. Using a pastry blender or two knives, cut the fats into the flour until the mixture resembles coarse bread crumbs with some pea-sized pieces of fat. Gradually stir in enough of the iced water until the mixture is moistened and begins to clump together. Gather up into a thick disk. Wrap in plastic and refrigerate for at least 30 minutes and up to 2 hours. (Pie dough is easiest to handle when it is cold, but not chilled rock-hard.)

2. Lightly dust a work surface with flour. Unwrap the dough and place on the work surface. Sprinkle the top of the dough with flour. Using a rolling pin, roll out the dough into a 13-inch-diameter round about ⅛ inch thick. Transfer to a 9-inch pie pan, being sure the dough fits snugly into the corners of the pan. Trim the dough to a ½-inch overhang around the edges of the pan. Fold the dough over so its edge is flush with the sides of the pan. Prick the dough with the tines of a fork. Cover and refrigerate for at least 30 minutes or up to 1 day.

3. Position a rack in the bottom third of the oven and preheat to 400°F. Completely line the dough with a round of parchment paper or aluminum foil. Fill the pan with pastry weights or dried beans. Place on a baking sheet.

4. For a partially baked shell, bake until the edges of the dough look set but not browned, about 12 minutes. Remove the pan on the sheet from the oven. Lift and remove the parchment paper with the weights. Pierce the dough with the tines of a fork again. Return to the oven and continue baking until the surface of the dough looks dry, but not browned, about 6 minutes more. Remove from the oven. Transfer to a wire cake rack. The shell can be used warm or cooled.

5. For a fully baked pie shell, bake until the edges of the dough look set but not browned, about 15 minutes. Remove the pan on the sheet from the oven. Lift and remove the parchment paper with the weights. Pierce the dough with the tines of a fork again. Return to the oven and continue baking until the dough is lightly browned, about 15 minutes more. Remove the pan on the sheet from the oven. Transfer to a wire cake rack. The shell can be used warm or cooled.

NESSELRODE PIE

For decades, Nesselrode pie was the ultimate holiday dessert, and it deserves a comeback. Named for a French diplomat of the 1850s who somehow became associated with chestnut desserts, it has a filling of candied fruits and chestnuts in a creamy, rum-spiked pudding. Make it for a holiday party, and it will probably become a tradition for you as well.

FILLING

¼ cup chopped candied fruit (any combination of candied green or red cherries, orange or lemon peel, citron, and/or pineapple)

¼ cup chopped marrons glacés, or vacuum-packed or drained canned chestnuts

¼ cup golden or seedless raisins, or a combination

2 tablespoons silver (clear) rum

1 cup half-and-half; divided

1½ teaspoons unflavored gelatin powder

3 large eggs, separated

¾ cup sugar, divided

⅓ cup heavy cream

Perfect Pie Dough (page 163), fully baked and cooled

TOPPING

¾ cup heavy cream

2 tablespoons confectioners' sugar

1 tablespoon rum

½ teaspoon vanilla extract

Chocolate shavings, for garnish (optional, see Note on opposite page)

1. Place the candied fruit in a wire sieve and rinse well under hot running water to remove the surface food coloring. Pat dry with paper towels. Combine the rinsed fruit, chestnuts, raisins, and rum in a small bowl. Set aside.

2. Place a wire sieve over a heatproof bowl near the stove. Pour ¼ cup of half-and-half into a custard cup. Sprinkle in the gelatin. Let stand until softened, about 10 minutes. Meanwhile, heat the remaining ¾ cup half-and-half in a medium saucepan over medium heat until bubbles appear around the edges. Whisk the egg yolks with 6 tablespoons of sugar in a heatproof medium bowl. Gradually whisk in the hot liquid. Return to the saucepan and reduce the heat to medium-low. Stir constantly with a wooden spatula until the custard is almost simmering and reads 185ºF on an instant-read thermometer (if you run your finger through the custard on the spoon, it will cut a swath), about 3 minutes. Do not let the custard boil.

3. Strain through the sieve into the bowl. Add the softened gelatin and whisk until completely dissolved, at least 1 minute. Place the bowl of custard in a larger bowl of iced water and let stand, stirring occasionally, until cold and just beginning to set, about 15 minutes.

4. Using an electric mixer set on high speed, beat the egg whites just until soft peaks form. Gradually beat in the remaining 6 tablespoons sugar and continue beating just until stiff and shiny, but not dry, peaks form. Whip the cream in a chilled medium bowl until soft peaks form. Fold into the custard. Stir about ¼ of the whites into the custard to lighten the mixture, then fold in the remaining whites. Let stand in the iced water until almost fully set. Stir in the soaked fruits and chestnuts with the rum. Pour into the pie crust and cover with a piece of plastic wrap pressed directly on the surface of the filling. Refrigerate until the filling is chilled and set, at least 2 hours or up to 1 day.

5. To make the topping, using an electric mixer set on high speed, whip the cream, confectioners' sugar, rum, and vanilla until stiff peaks form. Uncover the pie, and spread the topping on the filling, and top with the chocolate curls, if using. Serve chilled.

NOTE: To make chocolate shavings, use a 3.5-ounce bar or chunk of semisweet or milk chocolate. Using a swivel-blade vegetable peeler, shave curls from the short end of the bar, letting them fall from the bar over the filling. You may not use all of the chocolate.

DAIQUIRI LIME AND GELATIN MOLD

MAKES 8 TO 10 SERVINGS

There's something magical about food that shimmers as it shimmies. But when it comes to the perfect Jello-O mold, timing is everything. As a kid, it's darn near impossible to wait for the gelatin to solidify (usually, tiny testing fingerprints end up on the bottom of the mold). As an adult, it's critical to let the gelatin set just enough before you add the fruit or it will sink to the bottom (and hover embarrassingly at the top of the finished mold). A giant creamy, dreamy Jell-O creation that's spiked with rum? That we can wait for. (If you're serving kids, make sure to leave out the alcohol, or make them their own virgin version.)

Vegetable oil, for the mold
2 (3-ounce) boxes lime-flavored gelatin desserts
2 cups boiling water
8 ounces cream cheese, at room temperature, cut up
1⅓ cups iced water
2 tablespoons silver (clear) rum
1 (15-ounce) can fruit cocktail in heavy or light syrup, well drained

1. Lightly oil a 6-cup tiered gelatin mold. Combine the gelatin and boiling water in a heatproof bowl. Stir with a rubber spatula, occasionally scraping down the sides of the bowl, until the gelatin is completely dissolved, about 2 minutes. Add the cream cheese and whisk until the cheese melts. Add the iced water and stir until the ice dissolves. Stir in the rum.

2. Place the bowl in a larger bowl of iced water. Let stand, stirring occasionally, until the mixture has the consistency of unbeaten egg whites and is firm enough to support the fruit, about 20 minutes. Fold in the fruit. Transfer to the oiled mold.

3. Cover with plastic wrap. Refrigerate until the mold is chilled and set, at least 4 hours or overnight.

4. Run a dinner knife around the inside of the mold to break the seal. Dip the outside of the mold in a large bowl of warm water for 10 seconds. Dry with outside of the mold with a kitchen towel. Place a serving plate over the mold. Invert the mold and plate together and give them a sharp shake. Lift up and remove the mold. Serve the salad chilled for dessert, or in true Sixties fashion, as a salad.

FLAMING BAKED ALASKA

· · · · · · · · ·
MAKES 8 SERVINGS
· · · · · · · · ·

Hawaii isn't the only new state that inspired midcentury cooks. While various combinations of baked ice cream and custard existed as early as Thomas Jefferson's time, Alaska became the forty-ninth state, and baked Alaska became the dessert of the new decade. The dessert can be made well ahead of time, leaving you just a touch of last-minute decorating. And yes, you get to light it on fire! Choose your favorite ice cream, preferably one with an attractive color to contrast the pale meringue and cake. Better yet, layer two compatible flavors.

1 store-bought pound cake

1½ quarts ice cream, preferably pistachio, lightly softened at room temperature

6 large egg whites

¾ cup sugar, preferably superfine

1 egg shell half, carefully washed and dried

2 tablespoons brandy or Cognac, warmed, as needed

1. Line an 8½-by-4½-inch loaf pan with 2 overlapping sheets of plastic wrap, letting the excess wrap hang over the sides. (It is frustrating to try and use a single sheet to fit inside the pan, so just use 2 sheets to avoid using profanity.)

2. Cut the pound cake lengthwise into ½-inch slices. Cutting the cake to fit, line the bottom of the cake with cake slices. Spread the ice cream evenly and smoothly over the cake. Top the ice cream with more cake slices, cut to fit the pan. Cover the loaf pan with the plastic wrap. Freeze until solid, at least 4 hours or overnight. (The ice cream loaf can be prepared up to 2 days ahead.)

3. Position a rack in the center of the oven and preheat the oven to 500°F. (Give the oven at least 30 minutes to reach this temperature.) Cut a piece of brown or parchment paper a little larger than the top of the loaf pan. Place the paper on a baking sheet.

4. Whisk the egg whites and sugar together in the top part of a double boiler. Place over simmering water and whisk until the sugar is completely dissolved and the egg white mixture is opaque, foamy, and hot to the touch, about 2 minutes. Be sure that the egg whites do not begin to cook—the mixture should remain fluid. Use an electric hand mixer at high speed to whip the egg whites into stiff, shiny peaks.

5. Unwrap the top of the loaf and invert onto a work surface. Remove the plastic wrap. Transfer the loaf to the brown paper on the baking sheet. Transfer the tepid meringue (it will have cooled a bit) to a pastry bag fitted

with a 12-inch star tip. Pipe the meringue all over the top and sides of the loaf, masking it entirely. Do not pipe the meringue onto the baking sheet. Insert the egg shell, open side up, in the center of the top of the meringue.

6. Bake until the meringue is very lightly browned, 2 to 3 minutes. Use a wide spatula to transfer the loaf, on the paper, to a serving platter.

7. To serve, have a tall glass of hot water nearby. Pour enough brandy into the egg shell to fill it halfway. Dim the lights in the dining room, ignite the brandy with a long match, and make your entrance, sharing the spotlight with the baked Alaska. Let the brandy burn out of its own accord. Use a sharp, thin knife dipped in the water to slice the loaf crosswise. Transfer to dessert plates and serve immediately.

Light My Fire

Technically any dessert and almost any food, even ice cream and soup, can be flambéed. A few tips for perfect (and perfectly safe) pyrotechnics:

- **Never pour flammable liquid onto a lit fire or hot pan, as flames could travel up the stream of alcohol and set the entire bottle on fire.**
- **The liquor should be warm in order to flame properly. Warm it gently, just until barely hot to the touch in saucepan or microwave oven.**
- **Use a long match to light the fire.**
- **Make sure your food is in a flame-proof container (metal good, Styrofoam bad).**
- **The only liquor or liqueur you should use for flambéing are those that are 80 proof; brandy, cognac, and rum are good choices. Beer, wine, and champagne are bad choices. Anything 120 proof or over is downright dangerous.**
- **If you're pouring liquor over food to flambé, ignite it quickly so the alcohol doesn't soak into the food.**
- **You can contain the flames—and any residual liquor flavoring—by keeping them inside a "food cup": either half of an eggshell (carefully washed and dried), or half of a lemon (pulp removed). Press the cup into the center of your dessert, fill with warm alcohol, and ignite.**
- **For longer-lasting flames, soak sugar cubes in cognac or brandy. Ignite.**
- **If you wish, you can substitute an appropriate juice or nonalcoholic beverage for the liquor, but these cannot be flamed. Orange juice works well as a stand-in for orange liqueur, and apple juice is a good replacement for rum. You can also use juice with a dash of brandy or rum extract, although these usually contain alcohol.**

CREAMSICLE ORANGE AND VANILLA CAKE

MAKES 8 SERVINGS

This two-tone frozen dessert was inspired by our favorite ice pop, the orange and vanilla Creamsicle. Bake it. Take it. Share it. Love it.

Vegetable oil, for the pan
1 cup vanilla wafer cookie crumbs
3 tablespoons unsalted butter, melted
1 tablespoons sugar
1½ quarts orange sherbet; divided
1½ pints vanilla ice cream, as needed

1. Position a rack in the center of the oven and preheat the oven to 350°F. Lightly oil an 8-inch springform pan.

2. Mix the vanilla cookie crumbs, butter, and sugar together in a medium bowl. Press the mixture firmly and evenly into the bottom of the pan. Bake until the crust is set and smells toasty and sweet, about 10 minutes. Transfer to a wire cake rack and let cool completely.

3. Spoon about ⅔ of the sherbet into the cooled springform pan. Using your fingers (which will slightly soften the sherbet and make it easier to shape), spread it in the bottom and up the sides of the pan in a thick, even layer. Cover with plastic wrap and freeze until frozen again, about 1 hour.

4. Fill the center of the sherbet shell with the vanilla ice cream, again using your fingers, stopping about ½ inch from the top of the shell. Cover and freeze until firm, about 1 hour.

5. Using your fingers, spread the remaining sherbet on top of the ice cream. Smooth it with a metal icing spatula, making the sherbet flush with the top of the springform pan. Cover loosely with plastic wrap and freeze until firm, at least 2 hours or overnight. (The cake can be made up to 2 days ahead, covered and frozen.)

6. Let the cake stand at room temperature for 5 minutes. Remove the sides of the pan. Transfer the cake to a serving platter. Using a sharp, thin-bladed knife dipped into hot water between cuts, slice the cake into wedges and serve frozen.

SECRET INGREDIENT TWO-CHIP COOKIES

• • • • • • •
MAKES 2 DOZEN
• • • • • • •

These cookies pack a one-two punch. Mini chocolate kisses are the obvious star of these sweet-salty-crunchy-chewy cookies, but it's the crushed potato chips in the dough that will have you licking the bottom of the cookie jar.

1 cup plus 2 tablespoons all-purpose flour
½ teaspoon baking soda
¼ teaspoon salt
½ cup (1 stick) unsalted butter, at room temperature
¾ cup packed light or dark brown sugar
1 large egg, beaten
1 teaspoon vanilla extract
¾ cup crushed potato chips
¾ cup miniature semisweet chocolate chips

1. Position racks in the top third and center of the oven and preheat the oven to 375°F.

2. Sift together the flour, baking soda, and salt. Beat the butter in a medium bowl with an electric mixer until creamy, about 1 minute. Gradually beat in the brown sugar, and beat, occasionally scraping down the sides of the bowl with a rubber spatula, until combined, about 1 minute. Do not overbeat. Beat in the egg, then the vanilla. Gradually stir in the flour mixture with a wooden spoon. Stir in the potato chips and chocolate chips.

3. Using a tablespoon of dough for each, roll into 24 balls. Arrange on 2 large ungreased baking sheets about 1½ inches apart. Bake, switching the positions of the sheets from top to bottom and front to back after 6 minutes, until the cookies are barely beginning to brown around the edges, about 12 minutes. Do not overbake.

4. Let the cookies stand on the baking sheets for 5 minutes. Transfer to a wire cake rack and cool completely. (The cookies can be stored in an airtight container at room temperature for up to 5 days.)

CHERRIES JUBILEE

This cherry dessert was quite fashionable in the Sixties, perhaps because it was so easy to make (the hardest thing about it is scooping the ice cream) or perhaps because it was another opportunity to set dessert on fire: this time ice cream. To up the ante, use 1¹/₂ pounds Bing cherries, pitted, and about ¹/₂ cup sweetened cherry juice instead of the canned cherries, and sweeten to taste.

2 (15-ounce) cans pitted sweet cherries in syrup; separated
¼ cup sugar
1 tablespoon cornstarch
1 tablespoon unsalted butter
¼ cup kirsch (see Note) or brandy, heated until warm
Vanilla ice cream, for serving

1. Drain the cherries in a wire sieve over a bowl, reserving the syrup.

2. Measure 1 cup of the syrup and pour into a large skillet. Add the sugar. Sprinkle in the cornstarch and whisk to dissolve. Cook over medium heat, whisking often, until the mixture is thickened and simmering. Add the cherries and reduce the heat to medium-low. Simmer, stirring occasionally, until the cherries are heated through. (If using a chafing dish, make on the stove in the kitchen to this point. When ready to serve, reheat and bring into the dining room with the other ingredients. Place the chafing dish on its holder and ignite the fuel.) Stir in the butter until melted.

3. Pour the warm kirsch over the cherries, but do not stir it in. Carefully ignite the kirsch with a long match. Let the kirsch burn out of its own accord, or tightly cover the pan with its lid after 30 seconds.

4. Scoop the ice cream into individual bowls, and top with the warm cherries. Serve immediately.

NOTE: Kirsch, also called kirschwasser, is an eau-de-vie (liquor distilled from fruits) made with cherries. Authentic kirsch is always expensive because it requires 40 pounds of cherries to make a quart. There are less pricey, and not as good, versions out there, but they will do for most cooking purposes. Do not confuse kirsch with cherry brandy or schnapps.

CRÊPES BARDOT

To give these flambéed crêpes their Sixties due, we are literally passing the torch from Suzette (a girlfriend of the Prince of Wales circa 1895) to Brigitte by rechristening these for Miss Bardot. The blonde French actress was a cultural influence on everything from the bikini and beehive hairdo to the Beatles and Bob Dylan (he dedicated his very first song to her). Here's another recipe for your chafing dish, if you, like BB, enjoy playing with fire.

CRÊPES

1 cup all-purpose flour
1 cup whole milk
3 large eggs
2 tablespoons unsalted butter, melted
¼ teaspoon salt
Vegetable oil, for cooking the crêpes

SAUCE

½ cup fresh orange juice
⅓ cup sugar
½ cup (1 stick) unsalted butter, cut into tablespoons, at room temperature
Grated zest of 1 orange
Grated zest of ½ lemon
¼ cup dark orange-flavored liqueur, such as Grand Marnier
¼ cup clear orange-flavored liqueur, such as triple sec or Curaçao
Vanilla ice cream, for serving
Fresh raspberries, for serving

1. To make the crêpes, process the flour, milk, eggs, butter, and salt in a blender until smooth, stopping the blender to scrape down the sides of the container with a rubber spatula as needed. Let stand at room temperature for at least 30 minutes and up to 2 hours.

2. Lightly oil a 7-inch nonstick skillet (measured across the bottom) with vegetable oil dipped in a wad of paper towels. Heat over medium-high heat. Pour ¼ cup of the crêpe batter into the pan and tilt to cover the bottom of the pan with the batter. Fill any holes in the crêpe with dribbles of the batter. Cook until the underside is golden brown, about 1 minute. Turn and cook the other side. Transfer to a plate. Continue with the remaining batter, separating the crêpes with waxed paper. You will have 9 or 10 crêpes, but the extras will provide "practice crêpes" or can be nibbled as a chef's treat. Choose the 8 best-looking crêpes. (The crêpes can be made, covered with plastic wrap, and refrigerated, for up to 1 day.) Fold each crêpe in half, and then in half again, into quarters.

3. Bring the orange juice and sugar to a boil in a large skillet over high heat, stirring to dissolve the sugar. Cook until reduced by half, about 3 minutes. Remove from the heat, and whisk in the butter, a tablespoon at a time. Add the orange and lemon zests. (If using a chafing dish, prepare the sauce to this point on the stove in the kitchen. Transfer the sauce to a chafing dish. Bring the remaining ingredients, with crêpes, to the dining room. Set the chafing dish over the chafing dish fuel and bring to a simmer.)

4. Pour the two orange liqueurs into the skillet but do not stir. When the liqueurs begin to simmer, carefully ignite them with a long match. Let them burn out of their own accord, or cover with a lid after 30 seconds to extinguish. Add the crêpes and cook in the simmering liquid, continuously spooning the sauce over the crêpes, until the crêpes are heated through but not falling apart, about 2 minutes.

5. Divide the crêpes and sauce evenly among 4 dinner plates. Add a scoop of ice cream and some raspberries, and serve immediately.

STRAWBERRIES ROMANOFF

When Princess Grace lunched with Jackie at the White House, chef René Verdon ended the meal with this sumptuous strawberry dessert. Re-create your own royal treat by serving with small, local strawberries if possible. And while Chef Verdon used candied violets to garnish his dessert, you can also use fresh unsprayed violets or Johnny-jump-ups from your summer garden (as long as they haven't been treated by pesticides). Another tip: freeze the serving bowls, as this will melt fairly quickly, especially in warm weather.

1 quart small strawberries, hulled (or use large strawberries, quartered)
2 tablespoons orange-flavored liqueur, such as Grand Marnier
½ cup heavy cream
1 tablespoon confectioners' sugar
½ teaspoon vanilla extract
½ cup vanilla ice cream, slightly softened
Candied violets (available at specialty food stores or online) or fresh mint leaves, for garnish

1. Toss the strawberries with the liqueur in a bowl, cover with plastic wrap, and refrigerate for 30 minutes to 2 hours.

2. Just before serving, whip the cream, confectioners' sugar, and vanilla in a chilled medium bowl until stiff. Mash the ice cream in another medium bowl with a rubber spatula. Stir about ¼ of the whipped cream into the ice cream, then fold in the remainder.

3. Divide half of the strawberries with their juices among 4 chilled glass serving bowls. Top with half of the whipped cream mixture. Repeat with the remaining ingredients. Garnish with the candied violets and serve immediately.

CHAPTER 7
EXECUTIVE COCKTAILS

> **"Don't make your drinks too weak, or your party won't be very lively. Neither make them too generous, or you will have a bunch of drunks on your hands."**
> —*James Beard's Menus for Entertaining*, 1965

While it might seem like they drank more in the Sixties, according to a 2008 study published in *The British Journal of Psychiatry*, people actually drank less. A lot less. Today, the price of alcohol is half of what it was in 1960, and per capita consumption has doubled.

Our perception of the Three-Martini Life might very well hail from the *way* they drank in the Sixties. Cocktails parties were glamorous, drinks were sipped from real glassware, even the swizzle sticks had panache.

Here's how to re-create the perfect midcentury celebration.

THE RIGHT GLASS

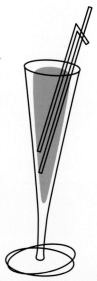

Do not take the one-size-fits-all approach. It is important to have the correct glass for the drink. This ensures a cocktail with the correct temperature and amounts of ice and mixers. Stock your bar with an assortment of glassware based on the drinks that you like to serve. Inexpensive used barware is available at secondhand stores.

Tall drinks served over ice with a large proportion of liquid mixers such as soda water, juice, or tonic such as Screwdrivers and Bloody Marys are served in tall highball glasses. (A "highball" is also a generic name for a tall drink made with liquor and a sparkling mixer,

such as soda or ginger ale.) Short drinks, usually served over ice with a small addition of mixer, are best in the short, stocky "old-fashioned" glasses, so-called because they are made to hold the cocktail of the same name. Tiki-style drinks should be served over copious amount of ice, so search out large glasses with tropical motifs, or use hourglass-shaped hurricane glasses (that average a 10- to 14-ounce capacity).

Cocktail (a.k.a. martini) glasses are used to serve drinks that are served straight up (that is, chilled but drunk without ice cubes). Today's cocktail glass is huge, and can hold up to 10 ounces. However, the traditional cocktail glass has a much smaller capacity of around 5 ounces. Smaller is better here, because the drink will maintain its chill during drinking. The drinks in this book are designed for traditional glasses. If you insist on serving in oversized glasses (a sure way to overlubricate your guests), you will have to experiment with the measurements to fill the glass. A saucer-shaped champagne coupe can do double-duty as a cocktail glass. Always chill cocktail glasses before filling in the freezer or refrigerator. You can also chill them by filling the glasses with ice and a little water, but empty and dry the glasses well before using.

MEASURE BY MEASURE

The single most important thing that you can do to make better drinks is to use a jigger for measuring the spirits. (You may see a bartender free-pour the liquor, but they do it for a living. Nonprofessionals should measure.)

A "jigger" is both a unit of measure for liquor (1½ ounces or 3 tablespoons) and the name of the small measuring tool used by bartenders. The latter comes in varying sizes, usually with two stainless steel cups conjoined at the bottom, although there are single glass jiggers with gradations marked on the side. The most useful size combination is 1½ ounce (1 jigger) and 1 ounce (1 "pony" or 2 tablespoons). When a recipe calls for ¾ or ½ ounce, just half fill the appropriate size. While you may see old cocktail formulas that call for jiggers and ponies, contemporary recipes use ounces. For large measurements of mixers, just use a regular 1-cup glass measuring cup; a set of measuring spoons comes in handy for small amounts of flavorings.

SWEETEN IT UP

Many cocktails include sugar, which was used by early bartenders to help smooth out the rough edges of rot-gut booze. Be sure to use superfine (also called bartenders') sugar, readily available in supermarkets. This sugar's fine crystallization easily dissolves in liquids. If you really want to improve your bartender skills, use simple syrup instead of sugar. Simple syrup is a liquid in which sugar is already dissolved, but requires twice as much volume as sugar. (One teaspoon of bartenders' sugar equals two teaspoons of simple syrup.) You can buy simple syrup at most liquor stores, or make your own.

To make Simple Syrup, shake 1 cup each granulated sugar and water in a jar until the sugar is completely dissolved. Refrigerate for up to 1 month. Shake well before using.

BETTER BITTERS

Many classic cocktails are seasoned with a dash or two of bitters, an aromatic distillation of herbs, spices, and other botanicals. During Prohibition, when cocktail drinking was clandestine, bitters fell out of fashion. Now that mixology is flourishing again, so is the bitters industry; you can buy bitters based on lavender, fruits, and even tobacco. When making drinks at home, use Angostura or another all-purpose (sometimes labeled "aromatic" or "whiskey-barrel") bitters.

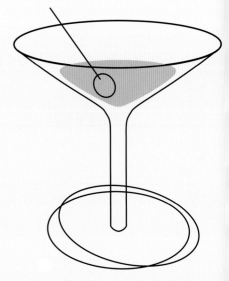

SHAKING VERSUS STIRRING

The *rat-tat-tat* of a drink being shaken in a cocktail mixer is a siren's call to liquor lovers. However, not all cocktails should be shaken;

many are better when the ingredients are stirred. Shaking effervesces the drink, a visual and textural effect that you may want for a Whiskey Sour, but would mar the crystalline look of a properly made Martini.

While there are no hard fast rules for when to shake and when to stir (many people find they have a preference after trying both), shaking is usually done to cocktails that include fruit juices, dairy, cream liqueurs, or other thick mixers. A shaken drink will appear cloudy in the glass at first, but will clear up. Stirring is usually reserved for spirits with light mixers to combine the flavors with a gentler dilution.

Professional bartenders usually favor a two-piece Boston shaker (a 1-pint mixing glass with a large metal canister that acts as a lid) because it's easy to clean quickly between orders. The three-piece cocktail shaker (a glass or metal mixing glass with a lid and lid cover) is a better choice for a home bar for its sleek look and efficiency.

To shake a drink, fill the shaker halfway with ice. Add the ingredients (liquor first, then mixers and flavorings), cover, hold with both hands, and shake at shoulder level for about 8 seconds. Don't shake much longer, or the ice will dilute the drink too much. Strain the drink through the lid spout into a chilled (or ice-filled) glass.

To stir a drink, fill the shaker halfway with ice. Add the ingredients (liquor first, then mixers and flavorings) and stir well with a long stir stick or bar spoon for about 10 seconds. Use a bar strainer (either a perforated julep strainer or a wired Hawthorne strainer) to hold back the ice and pour the cocktail into the chilled glass.

Shaken, Not Straight

Not all drinks that are mixed in a shaker are served straight up. Some are mixed with ice, then strained into an ice-filled glass—a seemingly redundant step that actually keeps the drink from diluting too quickly.

KEEP IT SIMPLE

When hosting a party, unless you have an Onassis-size bank account and bar space, it's best to keep the cocktail choices to a dull roar. Choose one or two drinks to offer your guests, memorize the recipes, and make those well. Some drinks, such as Bloody Marys, Tom Collins, and Mint Juleps, lend themselves to being made by the pitcher, which simplifies serving enormously. Leave the ice out of the pitcher and add the cubes to the serving glasses just before serving.

GORGEOUS GARNISHES

The right garnish, like a carefully chosen tie, will accessorize your cocktail with style. Be sure that citrus wedges and rounds are freshly prepared. For Polynesian-style drinks, stock up on little paper umbrellas and use ripe, fresh pineapple instead of canned. If you can, pass on the artificially flavored (and colored) Maraschino cherries and instead use imported Marasca cherries in syrup (easily available online). Choose plump stuffed olives for your Martinis, and top-quality jarred cocktail onions for your Gibsons.

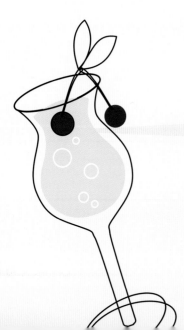

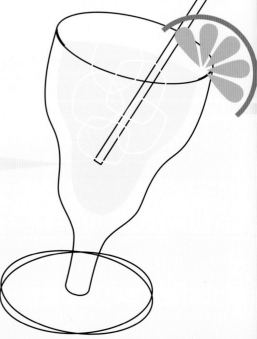

BLOODY MARY

Just a couple of decades before Sixties businessmen elected the Bloody Mary as the morning drink of choice, this cocktail was known as a Red Snapper. Here is a great formula for a nicely seasoned Bloody—make it hotter or milder, as you wish.

2 ounces vodka
4 ounces tomato juice
½ ounce fresh lemon juice
½ teaspoon prepared horseradish
¼ teaspoon Worcestershire sauce
3 shakes hot red pepper sauce
Freshly ground black pepper, for serving
1 lemon or lime wedge, for garnish
1 tall celery rib with leaves, for garnish

Fill a tall highball glass with ice cubes. Half fill a cocktail shaker with ice. Add the vodka, tomato juice, lemon juice, horseradish, Worcestershire sauce, and hot red pepper sauce to the shaker. Stir well (shaking can make the juice foamy). Strain into the glass. Add pepper to the top of the drink to taste. Perch the lemon on the rim of the glass, add the celery rib, and serve.

BLACK RUSSIAN

Equally tasty as an after-dinner drink or with nibbles at cocktail time, this caffeinated cocktail was enormously popular when televisions were black-and-white and ladies wore foundation garments as a matter of course. For an even richer drink, make a White Russian, as below.

1½ ounces vodka
¾ ounce Kahlúa coffee—flavored liqueur

Fill an old-fashioned glass with ice. Add the vodka and coffee liqueur. Stir well and serve.

White Russian: Gently flour 1 ounce heavy cream over the drink in the glass.

BLUE HAWAIIAN

As you shake this sky-blue cocktail, be sure to move your hips in an Elvis style. At this point in his career, the King was just a crown prince, as the previous generation's stars, such as Sinatra and Crosby, were the big names, and Presley was for kids. This is the kind of drink that gives tiki cocktails a good name.

1 ounce silver (light) rum
1 ounce blue Curaçao
1 ounce cream of coconut, such as Coco Lopez
2 ounces pineapple juice
Fresh pineapple wedge, for garnish
Maraschino cherry, for garnish

Fill a large tiki or hurricane glass with ice. Half fill a cocktail shaker with ice. Add the rum, Curaçao, cream of coconut, and pineapple juice to the shaker. Shake well. Strain into the glass. Garnish with the pineapple and cherry and serve.

Frozen Blue Hawaiian: Process the liquid ingredients with 1 cup cracked ice in a blender until smooth. Pour into a highball glass.

BRANDY ALEXANDER

A drink for people who don't drink, this cocktail is well on its way to being dessert. (In fact, its flavors can be turned into a pie, as described on page 158.)

1 ounce brandy
1 ounce white crème de cacao
1 ounce half-and-half
Freshly grated nutmeg or a sprinkle of cocoa powder, for garnish

Chill a cocktail glass. Half fill a cocktail shaker with ice. Add the brandy, crème de cacao, and half-and-half to the shaker. Shake well. Strain into the glass. Top with the nutmeg or cocoa and serve.

DAIQUIRI

MAKES 1 DRINK

The story goes that this drink, which offers the flavors of the Caribbean in every sip, was invented by an American planter in the wilds of Cuba's Daiquiri mountains in the late nineteenth century. Nowadays, you can make a frozen Daiquiri in a rainbow of colors and flavors, but the original was straightforward in its simplicity.

2 ounces light (silver) rum
1 ounce fresh lime juice
1 teaspoon superfine sugar or 2 teaspoons Simple Syrup (see page 180)

Chill a cocktail glass. Half fill a cocktail shaker with ice. Add the rum, lime juice, and sugar to the shaker. Shake well. Strain into the glass.

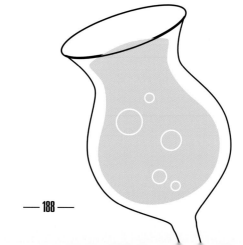

GRASSHOPPER

This cocktail has a strong feminine side, with a pretty green tint and a taste that is almost as sweet as liquid Junior Mints.

1 ounce green crème de menthe
1 ounce white crème de cacao
1 ounce half-and-half

Chill a cocktail glass. Half fill a cocktail shaker with ice. Add the crème de menthe, crème de cacao, and half-and-half to the shaker. Shake well. Strain into the glass.

MAI TAI

· · · · · · ·

MAKES 1 DRINK

· · · · · ·

Victor Jules Bergeron Jr., founder of the tiki restaurants that bear his nickname "Trader Vic's," claimed to have invented the Mai Tai when he had an overstock of rum. When he served it to a guest, the drinker supposedly exclaimed "Maita'i! roa!", a Tahitian phrase that loosely translates as "way cool!" Vic's rival Don the Beachcomber, the eponymous owner of his own Polynesian restaurants, also claims to have invented the Mai Tai, but of course, years earlier. Whoever it was, we thank them.

1 ounce aged or dark rum
1 ounce silver (light) rum
1 ounce triple sec or Curaçao
1 ounce fresh lime juice
1 teaspoon orgeat (see Note) or almond-flavored beverage syrup
1 teaspoon grenadine (optional)
Fresh pineapple wedge, for garnish
Maraschino cherry, for garnish
Fresh mint sprigs, for garnish

Fill a large tiki or hurricane glass with ice. Half fill a cocktail shaker with ice. Add the aged rum, silver rum, triple sec, lime juice, orgeat, and grenadine, if using, to the shaker. Shake well. Strain into the glass. Garnish with the pineapple, cherry, and mint and serve.

NOTE: Orgeat is a flavoring with almond and hints of vanilla and rosewater. Almond flavoring syrup also works well.

Yma Sumac

To make your Mai Tai taste even better and bring Trader Vic's into your living room, crank up some Yma Sumac. Generational Notes: if you don't know who she is, she's an exotic singer whose eerie voice was sampled by the Black Eyed Peas for their song "Hands Up." While there was a persistent rumor that she was really a Brooklyn woman named Amy Camus (Yma Sumac spelled backward), her claim to have descended from Incan royalty was supported by the Peruvian government.

MANHATTAN

While many think of the Martini as the ultimate New York drink, this one is the town's namesake. It has gone through some transformations over the years, mainly in the choice of its primary spirit. Rye was more obtainable in the Northeast (bourbon was mostly confined to the South), so whiskey meant rye. Use bourbon if you wish, or for a Rob Roy, get out the Scotch.

2 ounces rye or bourbon whiskey
1 ounce sweet vermouth
2 or 3 dashes aromatic bitters, such as Angostura
Maraschino cherry, for garnish

Chill a cocktail glass. Half fill a cocktail shaker with ice. Add the whiskey, vermouth, and bitters. Strain into the glass. Add the cherry and serve.

Dry Manhattan: Substitute dry vermouth for the sweet vermouth. Omit the cherry and garnish the drink with a green olive.

Perfect Manhattan: Use 2 ounces whiskey and ½ ounce each dry vermouth and sweet vermouth. Garnish with a lemon zest twist.

Manhattan, on the Rocks: Shake the drink and strain into an ice-filled old-fashioned glass.

Rob Roy: Substitute Scotch whiskey for the rye or bourbon.

MINT JULEP

The grand lady of Southern libations, many liberties have been taken with her. The drink should be served in a silver cup, which is not a standard item in a Yankee home, so you are allowed to use an old-fashioned glass. The main thing to remember is that mint is used as a fragrant garnish, and not a flavoring.

3 ounces bourbon
½ teaspoon superfine sugar or 1 teaspoon Simple Syrup (see page 180)
Fresh mint sprigs, for garnish

Fill a silver julep cup or old-fashioned glass with ice. Pour in the bourbon and sugar. Stir well, without touching the glass, to frost the exterior. Add a splash of water and stir again. Stand a generous amount of mint sprigs in the glass so the tops rise an inch or two above the glass rim. Serve.

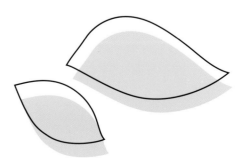

MARTINI

Of all the cocktails that have evolved over the years, the Martini has had the biggest metamorphosis. Until the 1950s, a Martini was always made with gin (in its original incarnation, the gin was sweetened) and a healthy dose of sweet (not always dry) vermouth. As expense accounts got bigger on Madison Avenue, so did the Martinis, and the vermouth (dry or sweet), with its lower alcohol content, only got in the way of the attitude-enhancing qualities of the vodka. Here's how a Mad Man would make a Martini. (And don't forget the Martini's cousin, the Gibson.)

½ teaspoon dry vermouth
3 ounces vodka
Pimiento-stuffed green olive, for garnish

Chill a cocktail glass. Pour the vermouth into the glass, swirl it around to coat the inside of the glass, and pour out the vermouth. Half fill a cocktail shaker or martini pitcher with ice. Add the vodka to the shaker and stir well. Strain into the glass. Add the olive and serve.

Gibson: Substitute a cocktail onion or two for the olive.

Martini, Dry: Increase the vermouth to 1 teaspoon, add to the cocktail shaker and do not discard. Add the vodka, stir, and strain.

Martini, Wet: Increase the vermouth to ½ ounce, add to the cocktail shaker and do not discard. Add the vodka, stir, and strain.

Martini, on the Rocks: Shake the drink and strain into an ice-filled old-fashioned glass.

The Three-Martini Lunch

In the Sixties, it was not only okay to drink on the job, in some cases it was encouraged. Businessmen—particularly those in sales and advertising—used long, alcohol-fueled luncheons with clients to close big deals and nurture important accounts. The practice was so common it had a name: "the Three-Martini Lunch."

While most company policies now bar employees from consuming any alcohol while on the job for a multitude of reasons—safety, health, and productivity—the real impetus for change might have been financial. In the Sixties, 100 percent of the business lunch, including transportation costs to and from, was tax deductible. In 1976, presidential hopeful Jimmy Carter found the practice to be unfair to the working class. He campaigned to end the government's subsidization of "the $50 martini lunch." Incumbent President Gerald Ford responded with a passionate defense: "The three-martini lunch is the epitome of American efficiency. Where else can you get an earful, a bellyful, and a snootful at the same time?"

Carter won, the business lunch tax deduction was whittled down—it was decreased to 50 percent in 1993—and the Three-Martini Lunch all but disappeared, until 2009 when the Palm restaurants unveiled an official "*Mad Men* Three-Martini Lunch." Cheers!

NEGRONI

Cocktails are an American invention, but the Negroni was born in Italy. A bittersweet combination of three European libations, it is just the drink to serve when you are feeling cosmopolitan. (Note that the cocktail we know as the Cosmopolitan didn't arrive until the Eighties.) Some people like their Negroni on the rocks.

1½ ounces Campari
1½ ounces sweet vermouth
1½ ounces gin
Orange zest twist, for garnish

Chill a cocktail glass. Half fill a cocktail shaker with ice. Add the Campari, sweet vermouth, and gin. Shake well. Strain into the glass. Rub the orange zest around the rim of the glass, twist over the drink, and drop it into the glass. Serve.

Negroni on the Rocks: Strain the shaken drink into an ice-filled glass and garnish with the orange zest.

OLD-FASHIONED

It's called an Old-Fashioned because it is the original cocktail recipe: whiskey, sugar, and bitters. If it didn't have these three ingredients, then it would be a toddy, sling, or another name according to the drink's formula. To make the granddaddy of all mixed drinks, start by crushing a sugar cube in the glass with some bitters. (This job goes much easier if you have a muddler, which looks like a small baseball bat, to do the crushing.) Although today many bartenders would muddle the cherry and orange garnish with the sugar before adding the liquor, in the Sixties, the fruits were strictly garnishes.

1 sugar cube
2 or 3 dashes of aromatic bitters, such as Angostura
2½ ounces rye or bourbon whiskey
Soda water (optional)
Orange slice, for garnish
Maraschino cherry, for garnish
Lemon zest twist, for garnish (optional)

Put the sugar in an old-fashioned glass and moisten with the bitters. Crush them together with a muddler. Add the whiskey and fill the glass with ice. Stir well. If desired, fill the glass with soda water. Add the orange and cherry, and lemon twist, if using. Serve.

Swizzle Sticks

While sticks of various shapes and sizes, including those stripped right off trees, have been used to stir drinks for centuries, the economic boom at the end of World War II, the rise of advertising, and the invention of plastic molding turned the once humble rod into a rock star. By the Sixties, swizzle sticks were hot commodities. Initially only stamped with an establishment's name and address, swizzle sticks soon became elaborate, multicolored, creative collectibles. The happy drink accessories fell victim to budget cuts from the recession of the early 1990s, but thankfully, they are making a comeback. Pick up a pack for your Sixties party, or better yet, grab a collection of vintage sticks on eBay. They're amazing bits of history, great conversation starters, and unlike those tiny red straws, will actually move your ice.

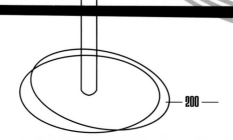

SCREWDRIVER

Many people are convinced that a morning Screwdriver, and not cereal, is the breakfast of champions. If you make this with freshly squeezed orange juice, you just might agree. Supposedly the drink gets its name because a crew of mechanics poured vodka into orange juice and stirred the brew with the nearest utensil handy—a screwdriver.

2 ounces vodka
4 ounces orange juice

Fill a highball glass with ice. Add the vodka, and then pour in the orange juice. Stir well. Serve.

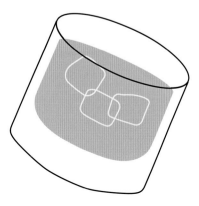

STINGER

You can make this bracing, minty drink with either vodka or brandy. When made with vodka, it's sometimes called a White Spider. It makes a hell of a mouthwash.

1 ounce vodka or brandy
1 ounce white crème de menthe

Chill a cocktail glass. Half fill a cocktail shaker with ice. Add the brandy or vodka to the shaker, and the crème de menthe. Shake well. Strain into the glass and serve.

TOM COLLINS

· · · · · · ·
MAKES 1 DRINK
· · · · · · ·

While you can buy prepared Collins mix with the other mixers at the supermarket, nothing beats a freshly made Collins with just-squeezed lemon juice. The drink was originally made with Old Tom gin, a sweetened gin. By the Sixties, vodka had replaced the gin. Try it with gin sometime (it doesn't have to be Old Tom, which has just returned to the market after years of unavailability), as it goes beautifully with the tart lemon.

2 ounces vodka or gin
1 ounce fresh lemon juice
1½ teaspoons superfine sugar or ½ ounce Simple Syrup (see page 180)
Soda water, as needed
Lemon wedge, for garnish

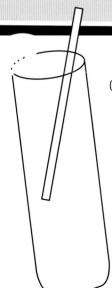

Combine the vodka, lemon juice, and sugar or syrup in a highball glass. Stir to dissolve the sugar. Add ice, and then top off with enough soda water to fill the glass. Add the lemon wedge and serve.

VODKA GIMLET

The current vogue for making cocktails is to use fresh citrus juice, but we firmly believe that sweetened lime juice cordial, such as Rose's, is essential for a proper Gimlet.

2½ ounces vodka
½ ounce sweetened lime juice cordial, such as Rose's
Lime wedge, for garnish

Fill an old-fashioned glass with ice. Add the vodka and lime juice and stir well. Add the lime wedge and serve.

Gimlet, Straight Up: Add the vodka and lime juice to an ice-filled cocktail shaker and stir well. Strain into a chilled cocktail glass, add the lime wedge, and serve.

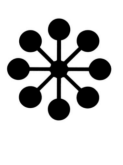

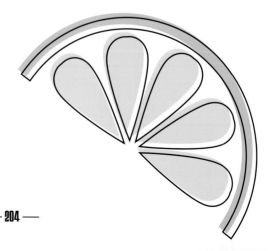

WHISKEY SOUR

The best way to mess up a whiskey sour is to use sweet-and-sour mix, a dubious product that has ruined many a cocktail. Stick with fresh lemon juice and some sugar, the whiskey of your choice, and you are guaranteed a puckery pleasure in a glass.

2 ounces blended Canadian whiskey or bourbon
½ ounce fresh lemon juice
1½ teaspoons sugar or ½ ounce Simple Syrup (see page 180)
Maraschino cherry, for garnish

Chill a cocktail glass. Half fill a cocktail shaker with ice. Add the whiskey, lemon juice, and sugar or syrup to the shaker. Shake well. Strain into the glass. Add the cherry and serve.

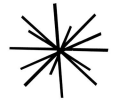

BON APPETIT!

The Sixties was a unique, almost magical period in American history: the bridge between old-fashioned glamour and modern technology, between traditional ideas and international influence. We would gladly return to the era of elegance when women wore pearls inside the house, men wore hats, and people got dressed up to get on airplanes.

There are so many things we love about it: the fashion, the feeling, the whole fabulousness of the decade. And hopefully now, everyone can add another item to their list: the food!

We hope you enjoyed our culinary trip down memory lane. As grand dame Julia Child, whom Rick had the distinct pleasure of knowing and Heather could only stalk from afar, would say in closing: *"Bon Appetit!"*

ACKNOWLEDGMENTS

I t was a wild ride creating THE MAD, MAD, MAD, MAD COOKBOOK. We would like to raise our martini glasses high to the following cast of characters:

Susan Ginsburg, our intrepid agent, provided services that you will not find in the official agent's handbook. Susan, there is a Purple Heart with your name on it. Also, to Stacy Testa, Susan's assistant, who kept us sane when things were at their most hectic.

The pitch-perfect photography is the work of photographer Ben Fink and food/prop stylist extraordinaire Libbie Summers. Both of these super-talents went out of their way to create the gorgeous photos. In fact, Ben went about 1,500 miles out of his way. We are forever grateful for your patience. And thanks to Brenda Anderson and Jessica Miller, Libbie's invaluable kitchen assistants; Fred Baily, who graciously provided our photo location; Andrea Goto, for looking so great in an apron; and George Woods, for lending us his dad's traveling bar kit. Many of the props were supplied by Habersham Antiques Market and Joel Snayd of ReThink Design Studio, both of Savannah, Georgia.

At Running Press, we are very happy to work with our editor, Jennifer Kasius. Thanks for keeping us on track with your customary grace and charm. We are indebted to our copyeditor, Susan Hom, and to Bill Jones and Melissa Gerber for the book's jacket and design.

Rick would also like to thank his kitchen associate and dear friend, Diane Kniss, for saving his neck again; Patrick Fisher, for stirring the Rob Roys; and Martha Foose and Joel Ruark for graciously supplying their recipes.

Heather would like to thank her mother Pamela Beach-Reber and stepfather Bob Reber for forcing her to watch "It's a Mad, Mad, Mad, Mad World" on cable countless times when she was little, and making her love all things 60s... including them.

A NOTE ON TRADEMARKS:

The following products mentioned in this cookbook are registered trademarks ®, and their use in this book does not constitute an endorsement or authorization by the owners of these marks:

7Up
Andes Mints
Angostura
Betty Crocker
Campari
Campbell's Soup
Cheerios
Cheez-Whiz
Chex
Coco Lopez
Creamsicle
Grand Marnier
Heineken
Heinz
Herbsaint
Heublein

Jell-O
Junior Mints
Kahlua
Kix
Knox Gelatine
Libby's
Lipton's Onion Soup Mix
Pernod
Pillsbury Dough Boy
Reddi-wip
Rose's Sweetened Lime Juice
Spam
Tang
Toblerone
Triscuits

INDEX

A

Appetizers, 17–48

    Blini and Caviar, 19

    California Dip, 29

    Clam Casino Dip, 20

    Coconut Shrimp with Hot Chinese Mustard and
Duck Sauce, 43–44

    Crab Rangoon, 22–23

    Deviled Eggs, 24, 25

    Flower Drum Song Barbecued Ribs, 36–37

    Oysters Rockefeller, 21

    Piggies in Blankets, 30, 31

    Pimiento and Walnut Cheese Ball, 32, 33

    Quiche Lorraine, 34, 35

    Real Onion Dip, 28

    Rumaki-a-rama, 39–40, 41

    Shrimp Cocktail with Bloody Mary Sauce, 42

    Spam and Pineapple Kebabs, 45

    Sweet and Tangy Meatballs, 26

Around-the-World Dinner, 97

Ashtrays, 9, 15

Asparagus aux Blender Hollandaise, 125

Aspic, 51–52

B

Baked Alaska, 168–169

Baked Chicken, Potato Chips, 99

Baked Ham with Soda Pop Glaze, 93

Bangers and Mash, 92

Barbecued Ribs, Flower Drum Song, 36–37

Bardot, Brigitte, 174

Barretto, Ray, 90, 91

Beard, James, 7, 178

Beef

    Beef Wellington, 74–76, 77

    Cold War Beef Stroganoff, 79

    Hungarian Goulash Gabor, 78

    Pan-Fried Steak with Butter, 80

    Piggies in Blankets, 30, 31

    Sloppy Joes, 67–68

    Souped-Up Swedish Meatballs, 89

    Spaghetti and Meatballs Sophia, 86–88, 87

    Sweet and Tangy Meatballs, 26

    Ultimate Meatloaf, 84, 85

    Yankee Pot Roast, 81–82

Bergeron, Victor Jules, Jr., 190

Better Crocker's Hostess Cookbook, 9

Birdseye, Clarence, 127

Biscuits, Homemade, 139, 141

Black Russian, 184

Blender Gazpacho, 58

Blini and Caviar, 19

Bloody Mary, 183
Bloody Mary Cocktail Sauce, 42
Blue Cheese Dressing, 54
Blue Hawaiian, 185
Brandy Alexander, 186, 187
Brandy Alexander Pie, 158

Breads
Buttermilk Dinner Rolls, 142–143
Date Nut Bread, 65–66
Everyone Loves It Stuffing, 138
Homemade Biscuits, 139, 141

C

Cakes and Cupcakes
Caramel Frosting, 155–156
Cherry Cheesecake, 146–148, 149
Chocolate Buttercream Frosting, 150
Creamsicle Orange and Vanilla Cake, 170, 171
Pineapple Upside-down Cake, 153–154
Rocky Road Cupcakes, 150–152, 151
Southern Caramel Cake, 155–156
California Dip, 29
Campbell's Soup Cans, 8, 62, 64
Caramel Cake, Southern, 155–156
Carter, Jimmy, 196

Casseroles
Chicken Divan, 102
Chile Rellenos Casserole, 123
Green Bean Casserole, 129
Macaroni and Cheese, 130, 131
Tuna and Noodle Casserole, 122
"Celebrity chefs," 6–7

Centerpieces, 13
Chafing dish, 14
Checker, Chubby, 91

Cheese
Chile Rellenos Casserole, 123
Fondue tips, 121
Matterhorn Fondue, 120
Not-from-a-Box Macaroni and Cheese, 130, 131
Pimiento and Walnut Cheese Ball, 32, 33
Potatoes au Gratin, 134
Secret Grilled Cheese Sandwich, 61
Cherries Jubilee, 173
Cherry Cheesecake, 146–148, 149

Chicken. See *also* Turkey
Chicken à la King, 106–107
Chicken Breasts Kiev, 104–105
Chicken Divan, 102–103
Miss Roaster Chicken, 98
Potato Chip Baked Chicken, 99
Soulful Fried Chicken, 100, 101
Child, Julia, 6, 34, 72, 98, 206
Chile Rellenos Casserole, 123
Chip-and-dip set, 14
Clam Casino Dip, 20
Clam Chowder, Manhattan, 57

Cocktails, 178–205
Black Russian, 184
Bloody Mary, 183
Blue Hawaiian, 185
Brandy Alexander, 186, 187
Daiquiri, 188
Dry Martini, 194, 195

Frozen Blue Hawaiian, 185
Gibson, 194
Glasses for, 178–179
Grasshopper, 189
Ingredients for, 180–182
Mai Tai, 190, 191
Manhattan, 192
Martini, On the Rocks, 194
Martini, Very Dry, 194, 195
Martini, Wet, 194
Mint Julep, 193
Negronis, 197
Old-Fashioned, 198, 199
Rob Roy, 192
Screwdriver, 201
Shaking, 180–181
Stinger, 202
Swizzle sticks, 14–15, 200
Three-Martini Lunch, 178, 196
Tips for, 178–182
Tom Collins, 203
Vodka Gimlet, 204
Whiskey Sour, 205
White Russian, 184
Coconut Shrimp with Hot Chinese Mustard and Duck Sauce, 43–44
Company food, 72–123. See also Main courses
Continental Cuisine menu, 114
Corn, Creamed, 126
Crab Rangoon, 22–23
Crab-stuffed Shrimp, 116, 117
Cream Cheese Sandwiches, 65–66

Cream of Tomato Soup, 62, 63
Creamsicle Orange and Vanilla Cake, 170, 171
Crêpes Bardot, 174–175
Crosby, Bing, 185
Cupcakes, Rocky Road, 150–152, 151

D

Daiquiri, 188
Daiquiri Lime and Gelatin Mold, 166, **167**
Date Nut Bread and Cream Cheese Sandwiches, 65–66
Deen, Paula, 140
Deep-frying tips, 44
Desserts, 144–177. See also Cakes and Cupcakes; Pies
    Brandy Alexander Pie, 158
    Cherries Jubilee, 173
    Creamsicle Orange and Vanilla Cake, 170, 171
    Crêpes Bardot, 174–175
    Daiquiri Lime and Gelatin Mold, 166, 167
    Flambé, 145, 169
    Flambéed Crêpes, 174–175
    Flaming Baked Alaska, 168–169
    Flaming desserts, 144–145, 169
    High-spirited desserts, 145
    Nesselrode Pie, 164–165
    Pineapple Upside-down Cake, 153–154
    Rocky Road Cupcakes, 150–152, 151
    Secret Ingredient Two-Chip Cookies, 172
    Soused Grasshopper Pie, 157–158, 159
    Southern Caramel Cake, 155–156
    Strawberries Romanoff, 176, 177
    Sugar Cookie Dough Crust, 146

Tart-Tongued Lemon Meringue Pie, 161–162

Tip Toe Inn's Lattice-Topped Cherry Cheesecake, 146–148, 149

Deviled Eggs, 24, **25**

Diat, Louis, 60

Dinner menus

Around-the-World Dinner, 97

Continental Cuisine, 114

Family-style Dinner, 83

Mai Tai Madness, 46

Mint Julep Jamboree, 132

Three-Martini Lunch, 160

Dinners, 72–123. See also Beef; Chicken; Fish and Seafood; Pork

Baked Ham with Soda Pop Glaze, 93

Bangers and Mash, 92

Beef Wellington, 74–76, 77

Chicken à la King, 106–107

Chicken Breasts Kiev, 104–105

Chicken Divan, 102–103

Chile Rellenos Casserole, 123

Cold War Beef Stroganoff, 79

Crab-stuffed Shrimp, 116, 117

Dinner Rolls, 142–143

Duck à la Orange, 112–113

Hungarian Goulash Gabor, 78

Lamb with Gravy and Mint Jelly, 94–96, 95

Lobster Newberg, 118–119

Matterhorn Fondue, 120

Miss Roaster Chicken, 98

Not-Quite Fish Sticks, 111

Pan-Fried Steak with Butter, 80

Potato Chip Baked Chicken, 99

Puerto Rican Pork Chops with Mojo and Onions, 90–91

Roast Turkey with Gravy, 108–109

Shrimp Scampi, 115

Soulful Fried Chicken, 100, 101

Souped-Up Swedish Meatballs, 89

Spaghetti and Meatballs Sophia, 86–88, 87

Tuna and Noodle Casserole, 122

Ultimate Meatloaf, 84, 85

Yankee Pot Roast, 81–82

Dips

California Dip, 29

Chip-and-dip set, 14

Clam Casino Dip, 20

Real Onion Dip, 28

Disney, Walt, 121

Dressings

Blue Cheese Dressing, 54

Green Goddess Dressing, 55

Red French Dressing, 55

Thousand Island Dressing, 55

Drinks. *See* Cocktails

Dry Martini, 194, 195

Duck à la Orange, 112–113

Dylan, Bob, 174

E

Eggs

Deviled Eggs, 24, **25**

Egg Salad, 69–70

Quiche Lorraine, 34, **35**

Salmon and Egg Salad Sandwich, 69–70, **71**

F

Family Dinner menu, 83

Fish and Seafood

  Blini and Caviar, 19

  Clam Casino Dip, 20

  Coconut Shrimp with Hot Chinese Mustard and Duck Sauce, 43–44

  Crab Rangoon, 22–23

  Crab-stuffed Shrimp, 116, **117**

  Lobster cooking tips, 119

  Lobster Newberg, 118–119

  Manhattan Clam Chowder, 57

  Not-Quite Fish Sticks, 111

  Oysters Rockefeller, 21

  Shrimp Cocktail with Bloody Mary Sauce, 42

  Shrimp Scampi, 115

  Stacked Salmon and Egg Salad Sandwich, 69–70, **71**

  Tuna and Noodle Casserole, 122

Flower Drum Song Barbecued Ribs, 36–37

Fondue, Matterhorn, 120

Fondue tips, 121

Foose, Martha, 155

Ford, Gerald, 196

Fried Chicken, Soulful, 100, 101

Fried Steak with Butter, 80

Frying tips, 44

Funicello, Annette, 91

G

Gabor, Eva, 78

Gabor, Zsa Zsa, 78

Gazpacho, Blender, 58, 59

Gelatin Mold, 51–52, 166, 167

Gibson, 194

Glassware, 12–13

Grasshopper, 189

Grasshopper Pie, Soused, 157–158, 159

Green Bean Casserole, 129

Green Beans in Mushroom Sauce, 128–129

Green Goddess Dressing, 55

Grilled Cheese Sandwich, 61

Grocery prices, 47

H

Ham, Baked with Soda Pop Glaze, 93

Hamm, Jon, 11

Heatherton, Joey, 6

Hors d'oeuvres, 17–18, 26, 38

"Hostess on Her Own," 9–10

Hostess tips, 9–12

Hungarian Goulash Gabor, 78

I

Iceberg Lettuce Wedge with Blue Cheese Dressing and Bacon, 54–55

Indiana, Robert, 64

J

Jefferson, Thomas, 73, 168

Johnson, Lyndon, 73

K

Kebabs, Spam and Pineapple, 45

Keeler, Brad, 14

Kennedy, Jackie, 72, 73, 176
Kennedy, John F., 49

L
Lamb with Gravy and Mint Jelly, 94–96, 95
Lattice-Topped Cherry Cheesecake, 146–148, 149
Lemon Meringue Pie, 161–162
Lobster cooking tips, 119
Lobster Newberg, 118–119
Loren, Sophia, 86
Lunch, Three-Martini, 160, 178, 196
Lunches
    Blender Gazpacho, 58, 59
    Cream of Tomato Soup, 62, 63
    Date Nut Bread and Cream Cheese Sandwiches,
    65–66
    Manhattan Clam Chowder, 57
    Secret Grilled Cheese Sandwich, 61
    Sloppy Joes, 67–68
    Stacked Salmon and Egg Salad Sandwich, 69–
    70, 71
    Vichyssoise, 60

M
Maclean, Heather, 206
Macmillan, Harold, 73
Mai Tai, 190, **191**
Mai Tai Madness dinner, 46
Main courses, 72–123. *See also* Beef; Chicken; Fish
and Seafood; Pork
    Baked Ham with Soda Pop Glaze, 93
    Bangers and Mash, 92

Beef Wellington, 74–76, 77
Chicken à la King, 106–107
Chicken Breasts Kiev, 104–105
Chicken Divan, 102–103
Chile Rellenos Casserole, 123
Cold War Beef Stroganoff, 79
Crab-stuffed Shrimp, 116, 117
Duck à la Orange, 112–113
Hungarian Goulash Gabor, 78
Lamb with Gravy and Mint Jelly, 94–96, 95
Lobster Newberg, 118–119
Matterhorn Fondue, 120
Miss Roaster Chicken, 98
Not-Quite Fish Sticks, 111
Pan-Fried Steak with Butter, 80
Potato Chip Baked Chicken, 99
Puerto Rican Pork Chops with Mojo and Onions,
90–91
Roast Turkey with Gravy, 108–109
Shrimp Scampi, 115
Soulful Fried Chicken, 100, 101
Souped-Up Swedish Meatballs, 89
Spaghetti and Meatballs Sophia, 86–88, 87
Tuna and Noodle Casserole, 122
Ultimate Meatloaf, 84, 85
Yankee Pot Roast, 81–82
Manhattan, 192
Manhattan Clam Chowder, 57
Martini, On the Rocks, 194
Martini, Very Dry, 194, 195
Martini, Wet, 194
Matterhorn Fondue, 120

Meatballs, Sophia, 86–88, 87
Meatballs, Swedish, 89
Meatballs, Sweet and Tangy, 26
Meatloaf, Ultimate, 84, **85**
Mint Julep, 193
Mint Julep Jamboree, 132
Movies from 1960s, 23
Music from 1960s, 16, 46, 83, 114, 132, 160

N
Napkins, 14
Negronis, 197
Nesselrode Pie, 164–165
Noodles with Sour Cream and Poppy Seeds, 133

O
O'Brien, Conan, 11
Old-Fashioned, 198, 199
Onion Dip, 28
Onion Rings, 128
Onion Soup Mix, 29
Orange and Vanilla Creamsicle Cake, 170, 171
Osmond, Donny, 49
Oswald, Lee Harvey, 19
Oysters Rockefeller, 21

P
Pasta
Noodles with Sour Cream and Poppy Seeds, 133
Not-from-a-Box Macaroni and Cheese, 130, **131**
Spaghetti and Meatballs Sophia, 86–88, **87**

Pies
Brandy Alexander Pie, 158
Meringue, 161–162
Nesselrode Pie, 164–165
Perfect Pie Dough, 163
Soused Grasshopper Pie, 157–158, **159**
Tart-Tongued Lemon Meringue Pie, 161–162
Piggies in Blankets, 30, **31**
Pimiento and Walnut Cheese Ball, 32, **33**
Pineapple and Spam Kebabs, 45
Pineapple Upside-down Cake, 153–154
Pork
Baked Ham with Soda Pop Glaze, 93
Bangers and Mash, 92
Flower Drum Song Barbecued Ribs, 36–37
Piggies in Blankets, 30, **31**
Puerto Rican Pork Chops with Mojo and Onions, 90–91
Rumaki-a-rama, 39–40, **41**
Spaghetti and Meatballs Sophia, 86–88, **87**
Spam and Pineapple Kebabs, 45
Pot Roast, Yankee, 81–82
Potatoes, Butter-whipped, 135
Potatoes au Gratin, 134
Presley, Elvis, 23, 185
Prices in 1960s, 47
Princess Grace, 176
Pupu platters, 38, 41

Q

Quiche Lorraine, 34, **35**

R

Real Onion Dip, 28

Red French Dressing, 55

Roast, Yankee Pot, 81–82

Roast Turkey, 108–110

Roaster Chicken, 98

Rob Roy, 192

Robinson, Smokey, 91

Rockefeller, Nelson, 21

Rocky Road Cupcakes, 150–152, **151**

Rodgers, Rick, 73, 116, 146, 155, 206

Ruby, Jack, 49

Rumaki-a-rama, 39–40, **41**

S

Salads

Egg Salad, 69–70

Iceberg Lettuce Wedge with Blue Cheese Dressing and Bacon, 54–55

Salmon Salad, 69–70

Tomato and Shrimp Aspic, 51–52, 53

Waldorf Salad, 56

Salmon and Egg Salad Sandwich, 69–70, **71**

Salmon Salad, 69–70

Sandwiches

Date Nut Bread and Cream Cheese Sandwiches, 65–66

Secret Grilled Cheese Sandwich, 61

Sloppy Joes, 67–68

Stacked Salmon and Egg Salad Sandwich, 69–70, **71**

Sauces

Bloody Mary Cocktail Sauce, 42

Hollandaise Sauce, 125

Hot Chinese Mustard, 43

Screwdriver, 201

Serving dishes, 11–14, 16

Shrimp, Crab-stuffed, 116, **117**

Shrimp Cocktail with Bloody Mary Sauce, 42

Shrimp Scampi, 115

Shrimp with Hot Chinese Mustard and Duck Sauce, 43–44

Side dishes. *See also* Vegetables

Buttermilk Dinner Rolls, 142–143

Everyone Loves It Stuffing, 138

Homemade Biscuits, 139, **141**

Noodles with Sour Cream and Poppy Seeds, 133

Not-from-a-Box Macaroni and Cheese, 130, **131**

Silverware, 12

Sinatra, Frank, 6, 185

Sloppy Joes, 67–68

Slow cookers, 14

Soups

Blender Gazpacho, 58, **59**

Cream of Tomato Soup, 62, **63**

Manhattan Clam Chowder, 57

Vichyssoise, 60

Spaghetti and Meatballs Sophia, 86–88, **87**

Spam and Pineapple Kebabs, 45

Spinach, Creamed, 136

Steak, Pan-Fried with Butter, 80

Steinem, Gloria, 9

Stinger, 202

Stockett, Kathryn, 155
Strawberries Romanoff, 176, **177**
Stuffing Everyone Loves, 138
Sumac, Yma, 16, 190
Swedish Meatballs, 89
Swizzle sticks, 14–15, 200

T
Table settings, 11–15
Tablecloths, 13
Thousand Island Dressing, 55
Three-Martini Lunch, 7, 160, 178, 196
Tiki culture, 23
Tom Collins, 203
Tomato and Shrimp Aspic, 51–52, 53
Tomato Soup, 62, 63
Toothpicks, 15
Tuna and Noodle Casserole, 122
Turkey. See also Chicken
    Roast Turkey with Gravy, 108–109
    Roasting times, 110
TV highlights, 49
TV Mix, Eat-by-the-Barrel, 48, 49
TV shows In 1960s, 91
Two-Chip Cookies, 172

V
Vegetables, 124–137
    Asparagus aux Blender Hollandaise, 125
    Butter-whipped Potatoes, 135
    Candied Yams with Marshmallow Topping, 137
    Creamed Corn, 126

Green Bean Casserole, 129
Green Beans in Mushroom Sauce, 128–129
Onion Rings, 128
Potatoes au Gratin, 134
Steakhouse Creamed Spinach, 136
Verdon, René, 73, 176
Vichyssoise, 60
Vodka Gimlet, 204

W
Waldorf Salad, 56
Warhol, Andy, 8, 62, 64
Watusi, 91
Wedding gifts, 16
Whiskey Sour, 205
White Russian, 184
Wood, Natalie, 90
Wright, Russel, 11

Y
Yams, Candied, 137